Endorsements

Within the pages of this fantastic book, Jackie Kendall passionately delivers with wit and wisdom a framework to help parents usher their princess into the arms of a committed prince, not a court jester. No fairy tales here, just biblical truth assisting dedicated families through discerning conversations and life skills which hold the potential to impact generations.

Michele Wetteland
Mom of five, children's author, and wife of
New York Yankee World Series MVP, John Wetteland

A ready resource for all moms as they cheer their daughters on to become girls after God's own heart. Jackie Kendall passionately equips mothers to fight for the hearts of their girls by sharing key principles which will guide their daughters to make good choices and wait for God's best.

DeDe Kendall
Elementary assistant principal and
co-author of *Lady in Waiting for Little Girls*

Jackie Kendall not only teaches this life message of how to guard your daughter from a Bozo and guide her to a Boaz—she also lives and breathes it with all of her inmost being and infectious energy. Jackie's passion, wisdom, and understanding, combined with her love for young women and her desire to see them walking in the truth of God's Word, propels this message in her newest book.

This is a must-read for every mom who desires godliness for her daughter!

Vicki Rose
Author, speaker, and Jackie's prayer partner for fourteen years;
wife of Bill Rose, Limited Partner of the New York Yankees;
mother and mother-in-law of two very precious women who waited

What a perfect read for the parent who yearns for a future Lady In Waiting! As a Christian therapist I regularly attempt to teach my single and divorced ladies to stop looking for Mr. Right but to use the "waiting room" time to focus on their own walk with the Lord. When a woman learns to love what the Lord loves, how could she help but be drawn to a Boaz who in many ways exemplifies Christ himself? And when she learns to love what the Lord loves, a Boaz couldn't help but be attracted to her—a woman whose eyes are fixed on pleasing the Lord. Only then can we see a true "love story from the Lord."

These are the principles Jackie so marvelously articulates in her book *Raising a Young Lady in Waiting.* Jackie's brilliant knowledge and love for God's Word, along with her love and devotion for the young women she serves, shines through each page. Parent, grandparent, child-worker—all will be blessed with the words in this book.

Kathy Martin
Author of *God and Psychobabble*,
licensed clinical social worker

There is simply no greater investment you can download into your daughter's life than the principles in this book! Having coached and counseled kids from the teens to the twenties for a quarter of a century, I assure you the anchor holds in these chapters. Besides that, I am living proof, having received one of Jackie's original manuscripts in 1988. No Boaz has had more prayer than mine. He has been well worth the wait, thanks to Jackie's teachings! As the pages turn you will find the time-tested skill set you need to design a Princess for King Jesus—a true Lady in Waiting.

Theresa A. Gernatt, "Coach Tag"
Former *Division I* basketball player and coach,
high school coach, and counselor

I am so excited for moms everywhere to read this book and begin teaching their girls at a young age the timeless message Jackie teaches in *Raising a Lady in Waiting*!

Having done Jackie's original *Lady in Waiting* study later in life, I can only wish that I had learned these principles at a younger age and avoided much heartache. I have lead the *Lady in Waiting* Bible study all over the country—with high school girls all the way to adult women—and have been blessed to witness the fruit in so many of their lives as they waited for their "Boaz," and are now raising children to know and love the Lord.

Kathy Edwards
RN Traveling Nurse in the NICU

Raising a Lady in Waiting is a must-read for *any* mom—but then again, I would read the phone book if Jackie wrote it! Her style of hard-hitting practicality mixed with insightful biblical truth always challenges me. Jackie has taken her *decades* of Bible study, mixed it with the time-tested truths she laid out in *Lady in Waiting,* and compiled them into an essential manual for every mom. This book will never make it to my bookshelf; it will stay prominently positioned on my bedside table as a constant reminder and reference point in raising my daughter to be a Lady in Waiting! The best part: I know that as I guide my daughter through the principles in this book, I'll be learning and growing myself!

Sami Cone
Founding blogger at SamiCone.com,
Nationally syndicated radio personality,
TV's *Frugal Mom*, author and conference speaker

As a mother of two young daughters, and a college softball coach, I am thankful that Jackie Kendall has put to pen what the Lord has laid on her heart to provide a resource to help us encourage our daughters to seek after God's best for their lives. Through the pages of this book, women will learn practical ways on how to empower their daughters to boldly pursue a man who will treat them with love and respect, and will truly be their Boaz. I married my Boaz seven years ago, a man of God who honors me and provides an amazing example of how a husband should treat his wife. I have seen how the principles of *Raising a Lady in Waiting* guide and inspire young women to wait for God's best. This book is certain to continue to positively impact lives for future generations!

Kimmy Bloemers,
Head softball coach for Palm Beach Atlantic University;
daughter of Hall of Fame baseball player, Gary Carter

RAISING A *Lady*

IN

Waiting

DESTINY IMAGE BOOKS BY JACKIE KENDALL

Lady in Waiting Expanded

Lady in Waiting (Revised)

Lady in Waiting Student Edition

The Young Lady in Waiting

The Right Guy for the Right Girl

RAISING A *Lady* IN *Waiting*

PARENT'S GUIDE TO HELPING YOUR DAUGHTER AVOID A BOZO

Jackie Kendall

DESTINY IMAGE® PUBLISHERS, INC.

P.O. Box 310, Shippensburg, PA 17257-0310

"Promoting Inspired Lives."

This book and all other Destiny Image, Revival Press, MercyPlace, Fresh Bread, Destiny Image Fiction, and Treasure House books are available at Christian bookstores and distributors worldwide.

For a U.S. bookstore nearest you, call 1-800-722-6774.

For more information on foreign distributors, call 717-532-3040.

Reach us on the Internet: www.destinyimage.com.

ISBN 13 TP: 978-0-7684-0323-7

ISBN 13 Ebook: 978-0-7684-8577-6

For Worldwide Distribution, Printed in the U.S.A.

1 2 3 4 5 6 7 8 / 17 16 15 14 13

Dedication

To my dearest friend, DeDe Kendall, who has an incomparable passion for the principles of *Lady in Waiting*.

Acknowledgments

First and foremost I want to give all praise to my Lord and Savior, Jesus Christ, who birthed this message in the heart of a college freshman and allowed it to grow into a lifelong ministry of warning others to not settle for a Bozo, but wait for a Boaz.

Ruth A. Olsen, my invaluable writing mentor—she has held up emotional "pom poms" cheering me on as I struggled to communicate my passion in print. In fact, Ruth has been my cheerleader through seven books. Only God knows her incomparable contribution to my "heart being in print."

Special thanks to the Destiny Image team that has championed the *Lady in Waiting* message for eighteen years, taking it all over the world.

My dear friend and mentor Bettye Galbraith who has prayed daily for this book project.

Last, but not least, my husband, Ken, who has been my Boaz for thirty-eight years and continues to be "a man worth waiting for."

Contents

Preface

A Fairy-Tale Engagement

When my Boaz was planning to propose to me, he wanted to do something unique and memorable. He put a lot of thought and effort into making our engagement one of the most treasured times of our lives together! To this day when I remember all the special details he attended to as well as the ways that the Lord blessed that beautiful night, I am overcome with gratitude—and no small degree of awe (but I will get to that later).

In this age of reality TV shows about over-the-top engagements and weddings, when high schoolers rent helicopters to stage the big "ask" to the prom, and first dates get taken to five-star restaurants, my story may not seem so extraordinary. But let your mind wander back to the mid-1970s when life was genuinely more simple and few American teens would have even rented limos for the prom. In *that* context, consider a college-aged young man who came out of a household of all boys and let me tell you what he planned and pulled off—all for the sake of getting to marry me! (Even typing that brings a lump to my throat.)

While we were home on break from our junior year of college, Ken made arrangements for us to drive to Disney World for the day. Just going to Disney World was a thrill for me—and is to this day! But Ken had much more in store than taking me up Space Mountain; he had called ahead and made reservations to take me to one of my favorite places in the world, Cinderella's Castle, and to a special restaurant inside the castle.

Can you even imagine how excited I was to walk through those doors and be escorted into the castle? I already felt like a princess with my attentive prince.

That was only the beginning of the night's surprises. After returning to the table from a trip to the restroom, our enchanted dinner was suddenly enhanced by a troupe of singing waiters, serenading us with songs about our love and delivering with a flourish a flaming order of cherries jubilee! As if this were not spectacular enough to this young woman in love with this wonderful young man, one of the waiters approached me with a beautiful book of poetry and declared, "A delivery from the prince of the palace!" It was a book addressed to "Princess Jacqueline."

And *then*, at what seemed to be the climax of this fabulous evening, our waitress asked, "Are you ready for me to take the picture?"

"What picture?" I blurted out, surprised again.

My sweet prince smiled at me and said, "She is going to take our picture out on the balcony overlooking the Magic Kingdom."

Well! If you think I walked, you'd be wrong, since I'm sure that I floated out onto that balcony. I knew full well that "no one" ever got to go to that special place—or, so it seemed—no one besides Cinderella waving at the crowds below. But there I was, and there we were, and before I knew it, the picture was snapped, the waitress departed, and Ken Kendall turned to me and asked me to marry him.

Was this really my life? For a girl from an abusive background, fairy tales and daydreams were a common way to disassociate from the painful world I lived in. How utterly ironic it was that in such a magical place, Ken would ask me to be his bride. How utterly fitting, as well. Walt Disney himself was raised in an abusive home and dreamed of creating a beautiful, fun, and safe place for families. Out of something painful in his life, he created something beautiful: Disneyland and Disney World. Out of something painful in my life, God was creating more beauty than I could imagine.

The very night of our engagement, God gave Ken and me a special bonus that shone with *His* beauty. As we left the castle, we both remarked about Jan, our waitress, and how open she seemed to spiritual things. She made several remarks during our wonderful dinner about her search for life's purpose. We shared as much as we could with her as she served our dinner, and now it seemed right to us to go back into the restaurant and tell her that we would love to talk with her more about this spiritual purpose in life that she was searching for. She accepted our invitation, said she got off work at 11:00 P.M., and told us that if we would come back, we could chat for a few moments.

Ken and I walked around the Magic Kingdom reveling in our brand-new status as an engaged couple, and anxiously looking forward to sharing with Jan about the reason she met us that night.

When we walked back into the restaurant, Jan actually came running down the stairs to meet us! We sat in the lobby of Cinderella's Palace and shared with her the hope that we both had found in Jesus. She remarked, "You guys were so loving toward me, I knew there was something different about you both."

So that night, Jan bowed her head and gave her heart to Jesus as Savior and Lord. When we hugged her good-bye and turned to walk away down Main Street, we both said at the same time: "We just got engaged and we just led someone to a personal relationship with Jesus!"

It was the *perfect* ending to this fairy-tale night. Talk about double joy! We walked out of the Magic Kingdom absolutely overflowing with joy.

As we drove back to West Palm Beach, we prayed that God would use our wedding ceremony as profoundly as He'd used our engagement on the balcony of Cinderella's Castle. Indeed, in His faithfulness and power, He did just that.

A man named Bill who was suffering with leukemia attended our wedding. He was so touched by our ceremony that he made a point to share his feelings with someone at the wedding reception. That someone was my mother-in-law.

As guests left the reception, Bill stayed behind and Esther Kendall explained to Bill how he could know Jesus intimately the way Ken and Jackie shared in their special wedding ceremony. Bill bowed his head that day and asked Jesus to be his personal Lord and Savior. Our prayer the night we got engaged was answered with Bill's decision to accept God's gift of eternal life through Jesus. Bill died two weeks later. He was ready for heaven, and God had graciously used our wedding as the setting for his eternal decision.

The Groom Comes for His Bride

The part of the wedding ceremony that absolutely rocked Bill to the core was when all the bridesmaids had arrived at the front of the church and it was time for the bride to walk down the aisle. The preacher stepped to the microphone and said, "Just as someday Jesus will come for His Bride, the Church, even so today, Ken comes for his bride, Jackie."

You see, my father would not come to my wedding. In fact, if you can even imagine it, he told me to pick a replacement for him. Somehow I was given the wherewithal to say to my abusive father that there is no replacement for fathers. Yet it didn't matter. He was completely unwilling to budge. So, Ken and I prayed about how to handle this highly unusual and very painful situation.

Here is what the Lord brought to our minds: Jesus Christ will someday return and come for His Bride, the Church. Then, this remarkable young man of only 24 years responded with an idea replete with the grace of God: "Jackie, I will come and get you and bring you down the aisle."

I am quite sure that neither of us had ever seen such a thing, but it was a work of God through the man He prepared to honor and care for me in this way. Not only did it display tenderness and touch the heart of Bill, but several of our friends from broken homes went on to conduct their ceremonies the same way. In fact, thirty-six years later, our own son walked from the front of the church to meet his precious bride and escort her down the aisle...another chapter in this extraordinary fairy tale.

Before you throw down this book in anger that you didn't have this "fairy-tale" engagement story, and before you roll your eyes, dismissing such a sentimental scene, I ask you to take a small glimpse at the backstory of my life.

The miracle of this whole experience, and of writing the best-selling book, *Lady in Waiting*, is the painful context of my life. I am the oldest of seven children, all sexually abused by our father. The fallout was horrible—including two suicides of my siblings and lives destroyed in myriad ways.

So, for me to learn in the Book of Ruth godly principles that guarded my heart and kept me from marrying a Bozo guy—that is a blessing I enthusiastically share with any woman who has a pulse! A nurse I once met said to me, "It is amazing to think that someone from your background would pick such an awesome husband."

Well, amazing and awesome are attributes of God, and surely *His* hand was the guiding force in my very ability to marry my Boaz.

Mom's Heart…Daughter's Schoolroom

Mom, as you seek the very best for your daughter's future, here are two wonderful realities: "The mother's heart is the child's schoolroom;"[1] and, "One good mother is worth a hundred schoolmasters."[2]

Too many parents assume that peers and media are the greatest influencers in the lives of their children, but this is absolutely not true. Consider the following survey results:

> An extensive study of 272,400 teenagers conducted by *USA Today Weekend Magazine* found that 70 percent of teens identified their parents as the most important influence in their lives. Twenty-one percent said that about their friends (peers), and only 8 percent named the media."[3]

You are the best teacher for your daughter, and it is Jesus who provides the best tutorials as we journey to raise godly girls. This book is a tutorial I was given that allowed me to cheer my daughter on to become a girl after God's heart and a young woman discerning enough to avoid Bozo guys and wait for God's best for her—her Boaz, her pillar of strength.

This book is for every mom. Whether or not you waited for your Boaz or even married a Bozo, your daughter can have a better dream. She can make good choices with the help of a wise cheerleader mom! This book is full of the nuggets of truth that God gave me as I prayed and even fasted for the life of our daughter.

I fear that the Bozo tribe is increasing; I watched many of these Bozo guys swarming around my daughter, even in a private Christian school. This book is the emotional "holy sweat" of one mom passionate about God's best for her daughter and the many other daughters God has brought into her life through decades of teaching these principles.

Introduction

***Lady in Waiting** is not about finding the right man,*
but becoming the right woman.
The Lady in Waiting
recklessly abandons herself to the Lordship of Christ,
diligently uses her single days,
trusts God with unwavering faith,
demonstrates virtue in daily life,
loves God with undistracted devotion,
stands for physical and emotional purity,
lives in security,
responds to life in contentment,
makes choices based on her convictions,
and waits patiently for God to meet her needs.

Who should read this book? Any mom with breath in her lungs who is keenly aware of the negative impact of our culture on our precious girls. Our culture encourages girls to put more effort into finding the right pair of jeans than the right kind of man. No wonder our daughters are falling for Bozo guys!

The principles in this book are intended to guard and to guide: *to guard* your daughter from a Bozo guy and *to guide* her toward a man worth waiting for—a modern Boaz. These principles have been taught for the last four decades to thousands of girls, who are now living their "happily ever afters."

> THE PRINCIPLES IN THIS BOOK ARE INTENDED TO GUARD AND TO GUIDE: *TO GUARD* YOUR DAUGHTER FROM A BOZO GUY AND *TO GUIDE* HER TOWARD A MAN WORTH WAITING FOR—A MODERN BOAZ.

Becoming the right woman: that is the goal. And the points laid out above are the framework for pursuing that goal. Each chapter will include a summary of a principle also found in *Lady in Waiting*. As a mother, I have grown in my passionate commitment to warn precious moms across America about the Bozo guys who would harm their cherished daughters. I would like to teach a million moms the transferrable concepts that are in this book, so that these moms can share them with other moms—moms who are intentional about protecting their girls from the soul-damaging impact of Bozo guys. The concepts in this book are "heart guards" for your daughter's heart and yours.

By way of clarification, I want to make a note about these young men I call *Bozos*. At no point am I dismissing the fact that they are *people loved by God* who deserve our kindness and prayers. We are *all* sinners saved by grace. So, my term is no indictment of a person; it's a caricature of the be-havior that we want to safeguard our girls against.

Bozos can be Christians or non-Christians, young or old, intentional or incidental in their motives; but they are still people Jesus died for. Truly the best thing a young lady can learn is to recognize poor behavior and see it as the signal to pray for a guy—*as* she asks God to give her wisdom in guarding her heart.

While you read *Raising a Lady in Waiting*, I hope you will find that there is a bonus for your heart. As you mentor your daughter in these life-impacting principles, you will also impact the girls your daughter will usher into your life. This book is a simple handbook for any mom interested in making an eternal impact on her child and all the other children who cross her path.

Ideal Mom—Former Prostitute

If by any chance you are a mom who thinks it is too late—be encouraged. The breath in your nostrils is proof of the hope that God is not finished with you *or* your daughter yet. I have done plenty of things wrong as a mom, so I was always inspired by the example of Rahab the harlot who not only converted to the true God of Israel, but also raised a most ideal son: Boaz.

Take a few moments to ponder the reality: Rahab, a former prostitute, raised a son who not only became the leading man in the love story of the Book of Ruth, but was also a pillar of strength and a man worth waiting for. Just read chapter 2 of the Book of Ruth. As you glimpse the godly characteristics of Boaz, keep in mind that his mama did not always make great choices. But her critical choice in Joshua chapter 2 changed not only her future, but yours and mine.

A former prostitute ended up in the Messianic line (see Matt. 1:5), and by God's grace, raised a Boaz, not a Bozo guy. In God's perfect orchestration, I truly believe that having been a former prostitute made Rahab even *more* sensitive to raising a son who protected a woman's sexuality rather than exploiting it.

Vital College Prep Course

Last year I began a Bible study called, "Tuesdays With Jackie". This study was on the campus of Palm Beach Atlantic University and was for girls only.

Beginning with the very first meeting, we addressed the issues these girls were facing in their everyday lives. As I began to listen to so many girls who were making such unwise and horrible choices, I wanted to scream! Where are the parents, and what are youth ministries teaching (or not teaching) our children?

PBA is a Christian liberal arts college, and I was stunned by what these girls didn't know. I wanted to cry out, "Are you unchurched? Did you participate in a church youth group? Did your youth pastor not teach you the *basics* about God's best for you or the guidelines for having a life more God-designed than Hollywood-created? Didn't your youth leader or your parents talk to you about not dating Bozo guys?" (I am worn out just writing about this outburst of indignation!)

I kept thinking about how we as parents are so concerned about our kids doing well in school and getting into the college of their choice. But here's a fact: I know too many kids who are passing school and flunking life in their relationships. Parents and youth ministries are failing to prepare our girls for the second most important decision of their lives. Of course the first most important decision is who will be their Master (in other words, their becoming followers of Jesus Christ). But the second most important decision of their lives is: who will be their *Mister?*

> I KNOW TOO MANY KIDS WHO ARE PASSING SCHOOL
> AND FLUNKING LIFE IN THEIR RELATIONSHIPS.

The best college-prep course is learning the timeless principles in the book *Lady in Waiting.* Now, certainly a mom can buy the book for her girl and hope that she reads it. But frankly, the book's impact will be magnified if a young girl has been introduced to the principles on a daily basis, with Mom modeling a growing love relationship with God.

"Cliff's Notes" for Mom

Knowing how full a mom's life is on a daily basis, I wrote this book as a summation of all that I have learned during decades of parenting and mentoring thousands of girls. I have read hundreds of books, so here is a compilation of all that I have learned, squeezed into one volume. In fact, you can consider this the "Cliff Notes" from my decades of searching for transferrable concepts to help mothers raise girls who will not become Bozo magnets. (At the back of this book you will see a list of the many books I have read—and it is not even complete!)

This book was born out of a genuine burden for every mom to learn the basics of raising a daughter who not only makes a difference for God in this world, but also attracts a Boaz rather than a Bozo guy.

The book is full of basic principles for you to teach your girl *before* she is attracted to the opposite sex. If your daughter is already "crushing" on a boy at school, this book is a must-read—before that crush crushes *her*. If your girl has already dated a Bozo guy who has broken her heart, you can begin to share with her the things you are learning to make sure she doesn't make the same mistake twice.

Guidebook for Paris, and Parenting

One of the greatest anniversary gifts my husband and I ever received was a trip to Paris, Prague, and London. One of our dearest friends gave us an invaluable custom guidebook for our time in Paris. It included maps, restaurant suggestions, daily special discounts at the famous museums, and details about when to go to each tourist spot.

Our friend even told us which meals to eat where in order to get the best discounts. She had lived in Paris, so she knew how to enjoy the city without running up huge credit card bills. Her maps were marked to show us exactly what walking routes to take from our hotel. Several people have made copies of this incredible personal guide to Paris.

When we were in Prague and London, we missed having the same great resource available to us.

I feel like *this* book will be a helpful tour guidebook as you maneuver through the challenges of raising a Young Lady in Waiting, and avoiding the tyranny of a precious child becoming a Bozo magnet.

You need to expose her to things that keep her standards high. As a parent/mentor, you're dreaming and praying for God's best for your girl. Most of you have such good girls that you're not worried about them. Well, let me tell you a little something. I had a good girl. I have a good girl. But I watched where I needed to encourage her to keep her standards high, to guard her mind, and to *not* settle. So I'm going to go over some things that I'm hoping you already know. In fact, I'm trusting that you know these things. But if you find yourself saying, "Well, I'll be honest, I did not know that," then, praise God you're here today.

If this were a classroom course for our girls, the key textbook would be my earlier book, *Lady in Waiting*. The book you hold in your hand utilizes the principles in the earlier book. It also expounds on them for the benefit of the mother/mentor/teacher.

The following quiz is just a pretest to clarify what you already know as a mother and where you may want a "refresher course." It will help you to examine your heart first so that you can discern more clearly the heart of your precious girl. The quiz also provides a glimpse of the topics to be addressed throughout the book; we will come back to each of these questions, in no particular order, in the pages ahead.

Prep Quiz for Moms

Key Question: Am I Prepared to Raise a Young Lady in Waiting? (Can I Help Prevent My Daughter From Marrying a Bozo?)

1. Do you know why older guys date younger girls?

2. Is your daughter growing in her love for Jesus, and does she see such growth in you?

3. Is your daughter experienced in doing for others? Does she help out at home and at church? Does she see this type of diligence in her mom, who is her first role model?

4. What is keeping your teen from doing for others? Is your teen too self-focused? Does she only do for others when it benefits her in the long run?

5. Does your teen have a No-Bozo Heart Guard? Does she understand the significance of getting her "seven" daily? (See Romans 10:17.)

6. Mom, did you know that sex ruins a good relationship or sustains a bad one?

7. Mom, did you know that that girls play at sex to get love and boys play at love to get sex?

8. Does your daughter grasp that if she will continue to pursue God's heart, she will attract someone who will encourage her to continue to grow—and they will be each other's spiritual cheerleaders? (See Hebrews 10:24.)

9. Mom, do you know what the "No Zone" is? Does your teen know about the "No Zone," and about staying out of it?

10. Mom, do you know why teen girls go too far? Would you know how to explain the law of diminishing returns to your daughter and her friends?

11. Do you know why so many precious girls marry Bozo guys? Did you know that sex blinds a girl to the Bozo she is dating or attracted to?

12. Do you know your daughter's "love tank" level? If her earthly father is absent, that love tank needs supernatural filling by her heavenly Father. Secure in Jesus, He must fill her heart deficit.

13. Is your teenager mildly content or an incessant whiner? Me-centric girls are "Bozo bait"...one selfish teen attracting another and wanting instant gratification.

14. Do you know how to be a "spiritual monitor" of your daughter's "crushing" on guys?

15. Does your teen carry (in her wallet or on her cell phone) a list of the qualities that describe Mr. Right?

16. Does your teen know how to avoid wearing chains on her wedding day? (See Second Corinthians 6:14.)

17. How patient is your teen? Waiting is a prerequisite for a "man worth waiting for"; impatience is the easiest way to be Bozo bait. (Worse than waiting is wishing you had!)

How did you do, Mom? Are you feeling encouraged or discouraged? Trust me; they are both good places to be, because they reflect a teachable heart. You purchased this book because you want to give your daughter the best available wisdom to impact the second most important decision of her life: who will be her Mister.

The key to raising a Young Lady in Waiting is to model godly characteristics yourself. If you read *Lady in Waiting* before you became a mom, you are probably very familiar with the list below; or, you may need a refresher course on these principles. When you as Mom conduct yourself as a Mrs. Right, it is easier to teach your daughter the characteristics of a Lady in Waiting. For now, let's take a look at the list:

- Being a Young Lady of Reckless Abandon
- Being a Young Lady of Diligence
- Being a Young Lady of Faith
- Being a Young Lady of Virtue
- Being a Young Lady of Devotion
- Being a Young Lady of Purity
- Being a Young Lady of Security
- Being a Young Lady of Contentment
- Being a Young Lady of Conviction
- Being a Young Lady of Patience

When you look at this list, does it make you smile with confidence or feel overwhelmed? This book will clarify each godly characteristic and encourage you as you encourage your daughter. The coming chapters will answer all the questions from the quiz you just took, and also offer "short visits" with Ruth that summarize each chapter's primary principle.

For those who have not read *Lady in Waiting*, I have two things for you to keep in mind: First, it is based on the precious love story between Ruth and Boaz. Reading the Book of Ruth (it's only four chapters) will enhance your appreciation for what you will read in *this* book. Second, each chapter of this book begins with a summation of a principle taught in *Lady in Waiting*. The summation will be helpful, but reading *Lady in Waiting* would be the most helpful.

One More Encouragement for Moms

Interestingly, I wrote this particular section *before* I began this book. I was already concerned that the reader would end up feeling like a failure after reading this material. So let's *begin* the book with the disclaimer I wrote before the Introduction was even in a rough draft form.

Disclaimer:

These words are meant to "throw cold water" in your face if by chance you are under the illusion that there exists some type of perfect formula for successfully mentoring your child. These pages simply describe the pilgrimage I have been on as a mom. I admit to all that I am simply a fellow struggler who is addicted to hope in Jesus. I am not attached to the outcome of my children's lives. But I *am* attached, or handcuffed, to Jesus, the only unchangeable reality on this earth. Our children have good days and they have bad years, but Jesus remains the same. Security is building your life around an unchangeable reality...Jesus: the same today, yesterday, and forever (see Heb. 13:8). As for our children: they are the same for a moment and changed for a while and hopefully spending forever with Jesus!

The best thing you can do for those you love so dearly is...*be intoxicated with Jesus!*

CHAPTER 1

Raising a Young Lady of Reckless Abandon

Ruth's Reckless Abandon

In the Book of Ruth, a young widow made a critical decision to turn her back on her people, her country, and her gods because her thirsty soul had tasted of the God of Israel. With just a "taste," she gave herself to the only true God by leaving her homeland of Moab and following her aged mother-in-law, Naomi.

Ruth abandoned the only life she had known. Some might call it reckless to leave one's people with no hope to be remarried in a strange land. But Ruth abandoned herself *to* something, and to *someone*. She recklessly abandoned herself to the God of all Creation.

> *But Ruth said, "Do not urge me to leave you or turn back from following you; for where you go, I will go, and where you lodge, I will lodge. Your people shall be my people, and your God, my God"* (Ruth 1:16).

Ruth had a determined heart. The Lord honored her faith in moving away from all that was familiar and taking a journey toward the completely unknown. Ruth did not allow her friends, her old surroundings, or her culture's dead faith to keep her from running hard after God. She did not use the excuse of a dark past to keep her from a bright future that began with her first critical choice: reckless abandon to the Lord God.

Foolhardy. Rash. Careless disregard. Withdraw support. Give up. Leave. Do any of these terms make you think of a right posture before God? They are synonyms for the words *reckless* and *abandon* that display the divine irony of our call to submit ourselves wholly unto the Lord.

The apostle Paul called himself a "fool for Christ." Jesus Himself "disregarded the shame" as He hung upon the cross (see Heb. 12:2 NLT). As daughters of the King who gave Himself for us, we are to give ourselves to Him, leaving the world, giving up our strategies, and withdrawing support from the wiles of the devil and the ways of the flesh. Reckless abandon is how we fling ourselves toward God and utterly forsake our sinful nature.

> RECKLESS ABANDON IS HOW WE FLING OURSELVES TOWARD GOD AND UTTERLY FORSAKE OUR SINFUL NATURE.

The "Shout 'Yes'" Mom

How does a woman display her own "reckless abandon" to God? Does she have to leave her family, hometown, and all her friends to prove such commitment?

Well, occasionally God might ask that of someone, but most of the time she simply needs to wake up in the morning and shout "Yes" to whatever the Lord has planned for her. (Now, if your family is still asleep, you may want to whisper "Yes" to Jesus.)

In his seminal work, *Mere Christianity*, C.S. Lewis described the opportunity we face every morning—and again and again throughout each day—to "get to the 'Yes'":

> It comes the very moment you wake up each morning. All your wishes and hopes for the day rush at you like wild animals. And the *first* job each morning consists simply in shoving them all back; in

listening to that other voice, taking that other point of view, letting that other larger, stronger, quieter life come flowing in. And so on, all day. Standing back from all your natural fussings and frettings; coming in out of the wind.[1]

This "shout 'Yes'" method may seem simplistic, but a teen girl who said "Yes" to God was given the privilege of being the mother of Jesus, our Messiah. Mary was not chosen by God because she was superior to all the teen girls in her neighborhood or youth group. Mary was chosen because God knew she would say yes. Here is a teenager's response to the angel Gabriel:

And Mary said, "Behold, the bondslave of the Lord; may it be done to me according to your word." And the angel departed from her (Luke 1:38).

In stark contrast to young Mary's "Yes" to a heaven-sent assignment, the Scripture tells us about an old priest who, six months earlier, struggled to say "Yes" to his miracle when talking to that same angel Gabriel (see Luke 1). An adult who was a spiritual leader resisted the prospect of the miracle God was promising—a child given in old age. And here was the consummate irony: because of his struggle and hesitation to say the word *yes*, Zacharias (also known as *Zechariah*), the father of John the Baptist, was struck mute until his miracle son was born.

And behold, you shall be silent and unable to speak until the day when these things take place, because you did not believe my words... (Luke 1:20).

The angel Gabriel spoke with an old priest and a young girl, and the young girl responded with reckless abandon to a most amazing and challenging assignment. Saying "Yes" to God is an act of daily surrender and a display of one's own reckless abandon.

Does your daughter know that you wake up shouting "Yes" to God? Is your daughter growing in her love for Jesus? Are you modeling such passion? Does your daughter have the courage to say "Yes" to God's plan over the pressure of her own agenda for her life?

Dateless Friday Night Miracle
(How to Avoid a Bozo)

Reckless abandon is a level of surrender that unlocks the greatest treasures God has in store for His kids. In fact, saying "Yes" to Jesus has preceded every miracle I have ever experienced during the past forty-five years as His follower.

> RECKLESS ABANDON IS A LEVEL OF SURRENDER THAT UNLOCKS THE GREATEST TREASURES GOD HAS IN STORE FOR HIS KIDS.

The very message that birthed *Lady in Waiting* arrived on a dateless Friday night in 1972. I said "Yes" to a holy nudge to stay in my college dorm room rather than go to the mall with some of my friends. I said "Yes" to time with Jesus in the Word, and I got an amazing miracle. Let me tell you about that miracle-producing dateless Friday night:

Before I became a Christian, I dated pretty steadily. Then I became a Christian and the pickings became rather slim. So, when I got a scholarship to attend a Christian college, I assumed that things would begin to pick up. How surprised I was to find myself dateless on several Friday nights! On the night already mentioned, my choice to stay in the dorm became like date night with Jesus.

As I sat in my room, my clothes were actually out on dates! Several of my cutest outfits had been borrowed so that other girls would look nice for their dates. In fact, a friend of mine got engaged in one of my favorite outfits. On her one-year anniversary, her husband asked if she could wear that cute outfit she wore the night they were engaged.

She replied, "Sure! Let me call Jackie!"

He was taken aback. "Why on earth would you have to call Jackie?"

"Well, if I'm going to wear that dress, I need to borrow it, because the dress belongs to Jackie."

Ha! My clothes were very busy in college—very popular, always on dates. I, on the other hand, wasn't nearly as popular as my clothes were.

So, back to that fateful Friday night. I was sitting in my dorm room thinking "Lord, I don't want to waste this time, and I don't want to feel sorry for myself. I need Your comfort. I need a word from You so I don't have to have these pity parties on Friday nights...Saturdays...Sunday afternoons—all the times I assumed I would be dating!"

Although I was a young Christian, I knew the best thing to do when you want comfort. It was not to go to the mall, overeat, or call a friend, but to open God's Word. So in the dorm room on my date with Jesus, I decided to read the Book of Ruth, because the chapel speaker that morning had referred to it as a love story and a story where a young woman broke her family's godless cycle and began a new life with the true God. In this precious little Book of Ruth, God showed me principles that became an outline for *How to Wait for God's Best.*

So what was so miraculous about finding these principles for avoiding Bozo as a life mate? The miracle was (and is) *me!* Here is how my family was described on the back of my book, *Free Yourself to Love.*

> As a survivor of severe childhood abuse, Jackie Kendall is an expert on forgiveness. A counselor deemed her family "one of the top-ten most dysfunctional in America." Though two siblings committed suicide and others adopted self-destructive lifestyles, Jackie wanted to break the mold and become a healthy, loving woman.

My severely dysfunctional background had prepared me to pick a *loser* (a Bozo)! Given my upbringing, my family example, and the context of everybody I ran with, my lover was destined to be one. But God took that "given" and gave me something else in its place. He gave me an outline of His principles to protect me from settling for less than God's best! And then He gave me the privilege of sharing those principles with other single gals. And *then* He gave me my very own Boaz. Many of you know this, but for those who don't, the key character, the leading man in the Book of Ruth is named *Boaz.* And, as you can see, if you change one little letter in his name, he can go from a winner to a Bozo.

God exchanged my prospects for a Bozo with the gift of my Boaz.

On a dateless Friday night, I said, "Yes" to a holy nudge to spend extra time with Jesus, and I was spared the "living hell" of marrying a Bozo. Instead, I have been married to my Boaz for thirty-seven years. Through the message in the Book of Ruth, I learned how to break my family's destructive cycle and embrace, with reckless abandon, God's best for me.

Prep Quiz Question No. 2: Is your daughter growing in her love for Jesus, and does she see such growth in you?

You know, the safest thing you can pray for and encourage your teenager to have is a *growing relationship with Jesus.* She doesn't have to be Billy Graham some day, or like his amazing preacher daughter, Anne Graham Lotz. She doesn't have to be the next Beth Moore. What I am asking you, Mom, are these questions: Can you tell if your daughter is growing spiritually? Is her heart open to spiritual things? If you can't say *yes,* you have a perfect prayer request. You know how to pray for her.

Moms, we pray for our kids to make the junior high cheering squad, but do we pray as passionately that they cheer on their own relationships with Christ? And do they cheer on their friends in their relationships with Christ?

> RECKLESS ABANDON IS HOW WE FLING OURSELVES TOWARD GOD AND UTTERLY FORSAKE OUR SINFUL NATURE.

Maddie and Libby's Story

How old does a girl have to be to encourage another girl spiritually? Some people think a girl has to be in high school to encourage a struggling best friend. Yet here's great news—there is no age limit on God using a young heart. There is no weight requirement or height minimum for the love of God to pour through the heart of a girl.

A grandmother I know tells a wonderful story of a late-night interaction between two BFFs. These girls were not seniors in high school; they were in elementary school! One night Maddie, who was ten years old, couldn't get to sleep because she was so anxious about having to move away from family and friends. She had lost her mom to cancer just the year before, which was the deeper source of her anxiety. Unable to sleep, Maddie texted her friend Libby and told her how anxious she was about moving. Libby texted back and told her friend to read James chapter 1, three times to help her heart calm down.

When I heard this story, tears filled my eyes, and joy filled my heart, because I know that God can use any heart that is growing in Jesus. Libby, at the age of eleven, had already been learning how to spur her friend toward trusting God rather than defaulting to anxiety.

And let us consider how we may spur one another on toward love and good deeds (Hebrews 10:24 NIV).

In three of the Gospels we are told how Jesus encouraged the people to allow the children to come to Him (see Matt. 19:14; Mark 10:14; Luke 18:16). He knew that children are open, teachable, pliable, and not cynically hardened by the world as yet. Our girls, from the moment they can speak and read, can be vessels used by God. Don't allow age to be a pass on God's using your child. Going into battle spiritually is for the mature, but a child can certainly learn to love and be kind and to serve God at a very young age—like Samuel who served in the Temple from kindergarten age forward!

I can't help but return for a moment to the story where the angel Gabriel told a young teenager that she would be the mother of the Messiah. Here was a teenager who simply responded to the angel's profound declaration: "You will be with child," with the most genuine question: "How can this be?"

The angel said, "What is impossible with men is possible with God."

And here's this little teen, "OK, then let it be. Whatever. I'm His servant" (see Luke 1:31-38). In the Living Bible version, Mary said, *"I am the Lord's servant, and I am willing to do **whatever** he wants. May everything you said come true"* (Luke 1:38).

I love that a teenager said "whatever" to God. Unlike its usage today, Mary's "whatever" was not sarcastic; rather, it was the reflection of a pliable, yielded heart. This teenager didn't say, "Are you *wacked*?" She simply said, "How is this possible?" And that was all right. It was a legitimate question. God loves our legitimate questions.

Your Daughter Pregnant With Messiah!

Your daughter is not going to have an angel tell her that she will be the mother of Messiah, but would your daughter have said "Yes" to such a pronouncement by an angel? Or is she a teen who would have been more worried about her parents' thoughts or the humiliation with her fiancé? Would she be more consumed by what she imagined other people would think about her than what Jesus thinks?

The safest place for your girl to be is the place where she is more concerned about what God thinks than what anybody else thinks—possibly including even her parents who may have dreams for her that God never dreamed.

Before Genesis 1:1, God had a plan for our children who know Jesus. This amazing plan is verified in Second Timothy 1:9, Romans 8:29, Ephesians 1:4-5, and Isaiah 25:1. Do you understand how strategically God has planned your life and your daughter's? His dream for both of you is so awesome!

Who walks in such dreams? Girls and women who grasp the secret of the alabaster box—a wonderful word picture for a Young Lady of Reckless Abandon.

The Secret of the Alabaster Box

In the days of Jesus, when a young woman reached the age of availability for marriage, her family would purchase an alabaster box for her and fill it with precious ointment. The size of the box and the value of the ointment reflected her family's wealth. The ointment-filled box was part of her dowry. When the young man came to ask for her hand in marriage, she would respond by taking the alabaster box and breaking it at his feet. This gesture of anointing his feet showed him honor.

One day when Jesus was eating in the house of Simon the leper, a woman came in, broke her alabaster box and poured the valuable ointment on Jesus' head (see Mark 14:3-9). The passage in Luke 7:36-50 that refers to this event harshly describes her as a woman in the city who was a sinner, marking her as one particularly wicked and reputedly depraved. But this broken woman found Jesus worthy of such sacrifice and honor that she risked even more public shame to perform this deed.

In fact, Jesus memorialized her gesture in Matthew 26:13, saying, *"I tell you the truth, wherever this gospel is preached throughout the world, what she has done will also be told, in memory of her"* (NIV). Can you imagine how angry people were that Jesus memorialized a "sinner"?

Way to go, King Jesus!

This broken alabaster box is full of great meaning. The woman not only unwittingly anointed Jesus for His approaching burial, she also gave her all to a heavenly Bridegroom. Yes, she was a sinner. Who isn't? (See Romans 3:23.) But this sinner had her dreams, and she wisely broke her alabaster box in the presence of the only One who can make a woman's dreams come true.

What is in your alabaster box? *What is in your daughter's?* Is it full of dreams begun when she was little, encouraged by the hearing of fairy tales about enchanted couples who lived happily ever after? Has she already broken her box at the feet of a young man who has not fulfilled her dreams, and has even broken some of them?

We all want our girls to hold on tightly to their alabaster boxes of dreams, each of them forever searching for the man worthy of the box's precious contents. Whether her alabaster box is broken or sealed shut, I encourage you to guide her in bringing it to the feet of Jesus.

The same is true for all of us. When you've placed your alabaster box at His feet, you will be able to respond like Mary to a heaven-sent assignment. When Mary was asked to become pregnant while engaged to Joseph, she did not argue with the angel. Her response was that of a woman who had already broken her alabaster box at the feet of Joseph and was now ready to take her broken box and lay it at the feet of a heavenly Bridegroom. She said, *"I belong to the Lord, body and soul..."* (Luke 1:38 Phillips).

I share the alabaster box story to encourage us as women to continually give our dreams to God and to encourage our daughters to prayerfully do the same. Dreams are the expectations of one's heart. Too often the expectations of our hearts become premeditated resentments when not given to God for proper guarding (see Prov. 4:23).

> Too often the expectations of our hearts become premeditated resentments when not given to God for proper guarding.

Still Grinning From a Date With Jesus

I told you about my Friday date night with Jesus in college. The fact is that I have never outgrown those special dates. Have you ever been on a date with Jesus? Several years ago, I realized that I had a totally free Friday night (all my family was out of town). I asked myself, "What are you going to do with your free night?"

As soon as I asked myself that question, my heart's reply was, "I can go on a date with Jesus!" So I went out to Singer Island and spent the evening sitting on a balcony eight floors up, waiting for the full moon to rise and enjoying a date with Jesus.

I brought along my Bible and journal and my prayer Rolodex. Just as I began to pray through some of the many prayer requests, I paused to look at the ocean, and suddenly I saw a rainbow. Now, a rainbow is not unique when it has rained—but it hadn't rained! I just gazed at that rainbow in awe and began to cry. Here I was, just beginning my date with Jesus, and He blessed me with a rainbow before the full moon came up. Talk about a double portion.

I started to think about what a rainbow represents—the faithful promise of the Lord—and I just cried thinking of the many promises that God has made and *kept*. I decided to look up all the references in the Bible relating to the rainbow and I discovered three men (Noah, Ezekiel, and John) who saw rainbows. Each of the rainbows was different, yet all three men had something in common—they faced hard circumstances. (See Genesis 9; Ezekiel 1; Revelation 4 and 10.)

As I thought about the rainbows that Ezekiel and John saw, I realized that their view was of heavenly status. The rainbows that we so casually look at are a reflection of a heavenly prototype, not merely a scientific wonder! I will never see a rainbow again without considering the rainbow that surrounds the throne of heaven (see Rev. 4:3) and heaven's rainbow of glory about the Holy One (see Ezek. 1:28).

On that high perch, with the bright moon lighting the beach, I pondered the gift God had given me that evening. What is it to experience the beauty of a rainbow without going through a storm? Here is what God showed me: *we can be rainbows of hope in people's lives even when they aren't facing storms.* Then, when their storms arrive—and they inevitably will—they will start looking for the rainbows of promise that speak to their hearts.

I raised my hands to praise the Lord for the rainbow insight, and suddenly that radiant full moon caught my eye again. I was captivated by it and thought about how far away it was and what effort, focus, commitment, passion, finances, and sacrifices were exerted to land men on the moon and plant an American flag there. As I pondered this, my heart began to grieve as I realized that men could pay such a *huge price to touch the moon* but were rarely willing to expend such passion to touch the heart of *the One who made the moon.*

When I consider your heavens, the work of your fingers, the moon and the stars, which you have set in place, what is man that you are mindful of him... (Psalms 8:3-4 NIV).

Driving back home from my date with Jesus, I opened my "full moon" roof and worshiped the Lord full throttle! What an amazing return I got on the investment of that one Friday night. How abundantly God met me on that balcony with a display of His splendor and ministry to my heart. Surrendering my "free" time to the Lord, my date with Jesus blessed me more than any trip to Target or night with Netflix.

When I raised my right hand through the roof in praise, I started to grin, realizing that at that moment my raised hand touched the heart of the One who gave me a rainbow while I was waiting for a full moon.

Raising Daughters Who
Listen to Their Heavenly Papa

In June of 1996, I heard Steven Spielberg being interviewed about his work with Holocaust survivors. He brought out a woman named Gerta, one of the few women who survived the Death March during WWII. The march went from Poland to Czechoslovakia; it was three hundred miles and three months long.

Gerta told an astounding story. She recounted that one afternoon in the concentration camp in Poland, she was told that all the women were going on a walk. Just before leaving, her father called to her across the courtyard and yelled, "Gerta, put on your boots!"

It was June and all the young girls were barefoot, including Gerta. But, being a good Jewish girl, she knew not to argue with Papa. So there was Gerta, putting on boots in June to take a walk, assuming, of course, she would return to camp.

This obedient young woman survived what turned out to be a three-month ordeal because she listened to her Papa. She watched the other girls breaking off their toes like twigs as their feet froze at night. Gerta watched hundreds die from their feet upward—as she survived in her boots.

What an extraordinary story of the simplest, yet most profound provision by God. Gerta's story is a challenge to all of "Papa's" children (see Gal. 4:6). Our heavenly Father knows the march we are on, and He alone knows what is ahead for each of us. So when He gives us instruction—even when it doesn't make sense (see Isa. 55:8-9)—we need to listen to Papa. This swift obedience is certainly part of our reckless abandon to Him.

Let's consider some basic instructions from Papa. Which of them are "boots in June" for you?

1. Love the Lord your God with all your heart, soul, and mind (see Matt. 22:37).

2. Love your neighbor as yourself (see Matt. 22:39).

3. Make the Kingdom of God your primary concern (see Matt. 6:33).

4. Be anxious for nothing (see Phil. 4:6).

5. Pray without ceasing (see 1 Thess. 5:17).

6. Be a student of the Word (see 2 Tim. 2:15).

7. In everything give thanks (see 1 Thess. 5:18).

8. Forgive as freely as you have been forgiven by Christ (see Eph. 4:32).

9. Esteem others more important than yourself (see Phil. 2:3-4).

10. Say "Yes" to God's script rather than clinging to your own agenda (see Luke 1:37-38).

Are you as challenged by Gerta's story as I was? Are you like Gerta when it comes to obeying your heavenly Papa? Or are you like too many of God's girls who would argue about wearing the boots and possibly start marching without the Father's guidance?

> OUR DAUGHTERS' TRAINED CAPACITY TO HEAR AND OBEY GOD WILL PROFOUNDLY IMPACT THEIR JOURNEY ON PLANET EARTH, AND HELP THEM TO DISCOVER GOD'S BEST FOR THEIR LIVES.

May we, as well as our daughters, be ready to obey and say "Yes" to Papa's instruction. We need to pray daily that our daughters will listen to and obey their heavenly Papa. Their trained capacity to hear and obey God will profoundly impact their journey on Planet Earth, and help them to discover God's best for their lives (see John 10:10).

Chapter 1: Questions for Discussion

1. Does the principle of reckless abandon seem too demanding for a mom, and even more so for her daughter? (See Ruth 1:16; Acts 20:24.)

2. Would you describe yourself as a "Yes" mom? By this I don't mean "Yes" to every demand of your child, but "Yes" to Jesus daily (see Luke 1:37-38).

3. What keeps you from a daily "Yes" to Jesus? Discuss C.S. Lewis quote already mentioned:

It comes the very moment you wake up each morning. All your wishes and hopes for the day rush at you like wild animals. And the *first* job each morning consists simply in shoving them all back; in listening to that other voice, taking that other point of view, letting that other larger, stronger, quieter life come flowing in. And so on, all day. Standing back from all your natural fussings and frettings; coming in out of the wind.[2]

4. Is your daughter growing in her love for Jesus, and does she see such growth in you? (See First Peter 2:2; Second Peter 1:3-9.)

5. Does your daughter have a "Libby" in her life who encourages her with the Bible when she is anxious? Is your daughter a "Libby" to an anxious and fearful friend?

6. Discuss your dreams for your life; discuss both yours and your daughter's need to break your alabaster boxes at the feet of Jesus (see Luke 7:36-50; Isa. 25:1; Rom. 8:32).

7. Have you ever been on a date with Jesus?

8. Discuss the story of Gerta listening to her Papa. Would you have listened? Would your daughter have listened? Look at the list of instructions from our heavenly Papa and discuss which instruction in the list would be "boots in June" for you?

CHAPTER 2

Raising a Young Lady of Diligence

Ruth's Diligence

Understanding God's promised provision for widows, Naomi sent Ruth to gather grain in the field of a kinsman. Ruth was willing to use her life to work diligently at whatever her Lord called her to do. She would not be paralyzed by her lack of a husband.

> *And Ruth the Moabitess said to Naomi, "Please let me go to the field and glean among the ears of grain after one in whose sight I may find favor." And she said to her, "Go, my daughter"* (Ruth 2:2).

When she and Naomi moved back to Bethlehem, Ruth did not waste a moment feeling sorry for herself. She went right to work. Instead of being drained by her discouraging circumstances, she took advantage of them and diligently embraced each day.

What more humbling work could Ruth have done than to gather grain for the survival of her mother-in-law and herself?

The leading man in the love story of the Book of Ruth is Boaz. This rich bachelor was attracted to Ruth not only because of her virtue; but also because of her diligence, the character quality she displayed while working in his field. Ruth was not afraid of hard work, and more than that, she was willing to work hard for the benefit of another person!

Boaz took notice of this very thing—that Ruth was working hard for her mother-in-law, Naomi, and not just for herself. Many young women are willing to work hard for something they have their eye on—expensive jeans, a trendy purse, or even a car. But, let's be honest here; working hard for the benefit of someone else is not always a strong motivator in the lives of young people. Diligence is dull in its curb appeal! So how do we, as mothers, encourage the development of this "less than appealing" character quality?

> **Prep Quiz Question No. 3: Is your daughter experienced in doing for others? Does she help out at home and at church? Does she see this type of diligence in her mom, who is her first role model?**

Humility and Diligence: Qualifications of a World-Changer

Ruth's diligence was manifested through her willingness to do what was required even when it wasn't—or didn't *appear* to be—the dream opportunity. Diligence fortifies a person with the capacity to continue long after everyone else has quit, either because the task was too hard or not satisfying enough.

Ruth was a young woman willing to do the necessary thing rather than the fun or glamorous thing. Diligence, ultimately, is the virtue of hard work versus "care-less-ness," as in, "I couldn't care less!" Sadly, I have encountered far too many young people who couldn't care less about the daily necessities of making life work or the background work for a project—and they are not afraid to wear that attitude right out front, like a bejeweled T-shirt.

> DILIGENCE, ULTIMATELY, IS THE VIRTUE OF HARD WORK VERSUS "CARE-LESS-NESS," AS IN, "I COULDN'T CARE LESS!"

This is what I call a "glitz and glamour" mentality that I have noticed more than once when I have tried to engage a young woman to help at an event. She is more focused on what will get her to the platform or keep her in the front row than on doing something behind the scenes—like passing out brochures or setting up the book table.

I read a comment in the best-selling book *Kisses from Katie* that addresses brilliantly what I have observed. I imagine the author would have admired Ruth's diligence and her willingness to do something so humbling. Here is what Katie said:

> People who really want to make a difference in the world usually do it, in one way or another. And I've noticed something about people who make a difference in the world: They hold the unshakable conviction that individuals are extremely important, that *every life matters.* They get excited over one smile. They are willing to feed one stomach, educate one mind, and treat one wound. They aren't determined to revolutionize the world all at once; they're satisfied with small changes. Over time, though, the small changes add up. Sometimes they even transform cities and nations, and yes, the world.[1]

Becoming a Young Lady of Diligence happens one small change at a time, not all at once! And sometimes it happens from the outside in. Sometimes we have to *do* the thing to *become* the thing.

These small changes will allow for the development of a "holy habit" of serving that will shape your daughter into a world-changer. The following activities are not difficult, and you can engage your daughter to participate until serving becomes second nature. Every time she does something for someone other than herself, you are shaping a Young Lady of Diligence.

Diligence and Internal Jogging

Although we may not think of it this way, prayer is certainly a form of service—perhaps the most important form. To pray is to pay attention to our relationship with God, to acknowledge our full dependence upon Him, which serves Him. Our intercession on behalf of others is also a service before God. Now, if you are anything like me, you have had to learn the discipline of prayer, since most holy habits do *not* just come naturally.

I once heard someone describe prayer as internal jogging. For those of us who have jogged or run (or in my case, done years of speed-walking), we know that to build up endurance and ability is a process. Our daughters are never too young to learn how to "jog internally." The prayer life of a Young Lady of Diligence can be life-impacting from a very young age. As with physical exercise, the only way to fail at prayer is to fail to show up.

> AS WITH PHYSICAL EXERCISE, THE ONLY WAY TO FAIL AT PRAYER IS TO FAIL TO SHOW UP.

Prayer is communication between two people who love each other. Very early you can teach your daughter that she can pray about everything: to take notice of God in her everyday life, to be thankful and grateful for faith and for kindness, and to confess when her heart or her words get off track. When life is difficult, the trials of her young life are perfect material for prayer: mean girls, crummy teachers, annoying boys, former BFFs, fears, hoped-for dreams, shattered dreams, family difficulties, and other things that make her the most anxious.

How often should a young girl pray? Hopefully you have modeled First Thessalonians 5:17, by praying continually. It is never too early to encourage that constant consciousness of our dependence on the Lord in *all* things.

In this generation when, more than ever, we hear terrible stories about bullying that can happen at school, after school, and *anytime* young people are engaged online, I hear a lot of questions about the "mean girls" at school. When moms bring up their legitimate concerns, the first question I have for them is: "How often do you and your daughter pray for these mean girls?"

Now, praying does not mean that a parent avoids talking to the school's leaders; it does mean that prayer is the *ultimate power* to handle not only mean girls but also every other aggravating, high-maintenance person who will cross our children's paths. In our home, whenever a difficult person was encountered we always said, "Now what do we do about a difficult teacher or fellow student?" And the answer was always the same—"Pray for them! Overcome evil with good!"

Do not be overcome by evil, but overcome evil with good (Romans 12:21).

A Holy "Hit List"

Does your daughter have a holy "hit list" in her Bible? This is a list with the names of other young people who need Jesus. It is a reminder to pray for them. I came to know Jesus personally through being on the holy "hit lists" of several teens. They were in a weekly Bible study and were encouraged to put down the names of the top ten kids at their school who they would love to see come to Jesus. I was one of those kids. Talk about a young person being a world-changer through prayer! That group of teens who prayed for me weekly changed my life for eternity. I was a lost girl from a majorly dysfunctional home, and God used *other teenagers* to pray me into His Kingdom.

When your daughter makes a list like this and prays for the kids on it, God will most likely use her in some way to be a witness to those very people. Praying for me week after week gave these teens the courage to ask me—week after week—to come to their youth meeting. Their diligence in prayer allowed them to never give up on me, even after I said no to their invitations at least ten times!

Teaching our daughters to pray for those who need Jesus is a *most* holy habit. We all have friends and relatives who need Jesus, and it is never too early to start praying with your child for the salvation of relatives, neighbors, and acquaintances.

Diligent Prayer for Her "Crushes"

Does that sound like a ridiculous suggestion to you? Let's think about this: Why *don't* we pray for the boys that our girls mention to us? We can be so quick to try to talk them out of a crush or, in the other extreme, to egg them on! Yet, since girls and boys are naturally attracted to one another in a God-given chemistry, the most important safeguard we can teach our girls is to guard their hearts through prayer.

When you think your daughter is "crushing" on a certain boy—then pray for him and ask her to pray for him. Such prayers are a wonderful "heart guard" for daughter *and* Mom!

Prayer is not merely preparation for a great work, it is the greatest work. Consider this: Daniel, one of the great prophets, was taken into Babylonian captivity as a very young man; but it is likely that, long before he was deported, his parents taught him how to pray three times a day!

...Three times a day he got down on his knees and prayed, giving thanks to His God, just as he had done before (Daniel 6:10 NIV).

Encouraging our young girls to be diligent pray-ers develops a foundational quality for all else a Young Woman of Diligence would seek to do.

Diligence and Holy Sweat

My husband worked for twenty years in short-term missions. The name for the behind-the-scenes servants on their trips was the *Holy Sweat Team*. The teens on these teams got up before anyone else to prepare breakfast, and stayed longer after meals to clean up. The Holy Sweat Team often missed out on some of the fun free time and other activities.

Would your teen *want* to be on such a behind-the-scenes team?

Let's pull back from the scene of a mission trip and consider how your daughter serves on her home turf. Is she learning how to clear the kitchen table without being asked? Does it take an act of Congress to have your daughter put dishes in the dishwasher? Some young people equate helping around the house with punishment...and in some homes it is presented this way. But you can reframe your daughter's view of helping at home (or in any environment) as a *blessing to others* and not a curse for her. In fact, working up a holy sweat of service is an offering to God—a "sweat offering" that will come back as a blessing upon a young person's own heart.

> WORKING UP A HOLY SWEAT OF SERVICE IS AN OFFERING TO GOD—A "SWEAT OFFERING" THAT WILL COME BACK AS A BLESSING UPON A YOUNG PERSON'S OWN HEART.

The same principle applies at church. Have you asked your daughter to help you serve at church, by including her in some form of service to others, like Vacation Bible School or a summer mission project? Maybe you serve in the nursery and she could help with those little ones. As she sees this type of diligence in her mom and is invited to join in, she will grow in this beautiful holy habit of serving in the church body. Remember Mom, you're her first and best role model.

Here is a great mother-daughter activity: read Proverbs 31:10-31 and discuss the qualities that make up a "P-31 Woman." When we consider the various projects the P-31 Woman was involved in, we know that her ability to engage with and thrive in these activities did not suddenly appear when she got married. We can be certain that the P-31 Woman was in training as a Young Lady of Diligence long before that!

> *She selects wool and flax and works with eager hands....She sets about her work vigorously; her arms are strong for her tasks* (Proverbs 31:13,17 NIV).

The strength and vigor of a P-31 Woman begins as a little girl, the first time she helps load the dishwasher or pick up the toys or helps cook a meal. All these strengths develop as a little girl stands side by side with her mother and shares a task or serves together at church or in their community.

I just read this recent example of a junior high girl making a difference:

> I am so proud of Ashten, newest member of the Cobra Club "Student of the Month." Comments from her teacher include that she is always positive and upbeat. She gets along well with others and she helps out wherever she can. She is a dedicated and aspiring student with a bright future ahead of her...12 years old...[2]

Notice it says of the twelve-year-old that "she helps out wherever she can." It sounds like Ashten's mom is raising her to be a Young Lady of Diligence. Could your daughter be a member of the Cobra Club next month?

Diligence and Breaking One's Piggy Bank

Another area of giving that a Young Lady of Diligence can develop is the ability to give money unselfishly for the needs of others. Nothing is more touching than to see a young person give of her limited funds to a needy cause—whether in church, school, or community.

When our daughter was in third grade, her class put together a care package for a missionary family in Japan. She came home and asked if we could go to the store and buy Banana Nerds and red licorice for the missionary children. I may have laughed right out loud with delight, imagining these children finding those treats in their packages—and even sharing them with their little Japanese friends. As an eight-year-old, Jessi's heart wanted to reach out and bless the children of the missionaries—and what better way than with her favorite candy!

When our son was in seventh grade, he had saved a pretty large sum of money that he wanted to spend on a special trip we would be taking at Christmastime. As the trip drew near, Ben found out about a financial need of his favorite teacher. He came home from school and told my husband and me that he wanted to give this teacher all the money he had saved, so the teacher could fix his broken car. We were so blessed by this godly desire that we actually were in tears as we told him how noble his choice was.

Girls and boys have such tender hearts. Isn't it our privilege to encourage such unselfish giving? The P-31 Woman certainly learned giving as a child, as evidenced by her generous giving as an adult. Proverbs 31:20 explains: *"She opens her arms to the poor and extends her hands to the needy"* (NIV).

Diligence and Hallmark Cards

What about the gift of encouragement? Sending encouraging cards to people has always been a favorite pastime for me. From a young age I have been keenly aware of the power of the written word to give fresh oxygen to another soul.

With the cost of greeting cards increasing to the price of what used to be the cost of a book, I may not send actual cards as frequently as I used to, but there are plenty of other methods to communicate words of hope, including e-mails, texting, and even phone calls.

Whether the encouragement is spoken or written, the ministry of encouragement is hardly reserved for adults only. Young girls can be an important encouragement to each other, even through thoughtful texting. Remember the story in Chapter 1 about Maddie and Libby? I am still touched thinking about how Libby's text message encouraged Maddie to read a particular passage of Scripture to help calm her anxious heart.

FROM A YOUNG AGE I HAVE BEEN KEENLY AWARE OF THE POWER OF THE WRITTEN WORD TO GIVE FRESH OXYGEN TO ANOTHER SOUL.

How often does your daughter hear you share an encouraging word to someone over the phone? How frequently does she see you writing out some Scriptures on a card to encourage a friend who is facing a difficult trial? Directing someone's attention to the hope that is in God's Word is a great ministry. The prophet Isaiah wrote out the perfect formula for this world-changing ministry of encouragement:

> *The sovereign* LORD *has given me an instructed tongue, to know the word that sustains the weary. He wakens me morning by morning, wakens my ear to listen like one being taught* (Isaiah 50:4 NIV).

Time spent learning God's Word allows any woman, young or old, to develop the "instructed tongue" so that she can direct a person's attention to the hope of God's many promises. You can even create an "anti-doubt" journal where you record all your favorite verses that have encouraged your heart on your adventure with Jesus. (We will discuss this more in Chapter 3.)

Whether e-mailing, texting, or even writing a card, God's girls can keep hope alive in the hearts of those they love—simply by being cheerleaders of truth! John Maxwell has said that "80 percent of ministry taking place in churches is done by women." Why? I know there are many factors that explain that statement, but I know one reason is that most women are not afraid of hard work. Women are not only ready to get their hands dirty but also to dive into the painful and often bewildering world of soul care for the many wounded hearts in our world. Diligent women model for their daughters the honor to be on God's team—helping to keep hope alive.

THROUGH ALL HER ACTIVITIES, THE YOUNG LADY OF DILIGENCE CAN HAVE A MINISTRY OF ENCOURAGEMENT. FROM A HOLY HUG TO A HALLMARK CARD, SHE CAN PROVIDE ONE OF HER FRIENDS, OR EVEN A SIBLING, THE "WILL TO CONTINUE" AND A REASON TO KEEP GOING!

"Hope deferred makes the heart sick, but a longing fulfilled is a tree of life" (Prov. 13:12 NIV). Dr. Larry Crabb has said, "Encouragement is the kind expression that helps someone want to be a better Christian even when life is rough."[3] The ministry of hope and encouragement spurs people on in the sanctifying journey of personal holiness. Part of the process of holiness is the will to continue even when life is rough. Through all her activities, the Young Lady of Diligence can have a ministry of encouragement. From a holy hug to a Hallmark card, she can provide one of her friends, or even a sibling, the "will to continue" and a reason to keep going!

Carry each other's burdens, and in this way you will fulfill the law of Christ (Galatians 6:2 NIV).

One Greek word for *burden* means "burdened under pressure, difficulty, grief, savage or fierce weight." Even our young teens can feel a kind of savage or seemingly ferocious pressure, whether at school from teachers and peers, or at home from difficult circumstances or relationships. As a teenager I certainly faced a savage and fierce weight that only Jesus could remove. He lifted this weight from me through my discovering one verse and its meaning: *"For we have not an high priest which cannot be touched with the feeling of our infirmities..."* (Heb. 4:15 KJV).

This is one of the first verses I learned as a young believer living in an abusive home. If I didn't believe that Jesus was touched by the feelings of my anguish, I would never have been confident enough in Him to keep following Him.

Now, here is the kicker: I looked up the word *touched*—oh my goodness! The Greek word for touched here is *sumpatheo*.[4] I am sure that word looks familiar to you, since we get our English word sympathy from this base. Here is what it means:

- compassion
- experience pain jointly
- touched with sympathy
- having fellow-feelings

To someone who's suffering, we can offer the exceptional good news that Jesus is *touched* by her painful feelings. Jesus embodies a *conjoined experience of sympathy and compassion!*

The depth of the truth in this particular passage has kept this woman "addicted" to hope in Jesus since I was a young teen. Along the way, many Ladies of Diligence so encouraged me through their good works that the "will to continue" flamed daily in my soul.

Diligence and a Junk Food Drawer

The next holy habit with which you can encourage your daughter is *hospitality.* You may be wondering how a young girl participates in hospitality when many adults don't take time to practice it. While the Bible holds up hospitality as a virtue to practice among the saints (see Rom. 12:13; 1 Pet. 4:9), as well as a requirement for spiritual leaders (see Titus 1:8), it is ministry less and less practiced in our fast-paced society.

So how do our daughters learn hospitality? Well, Mom, you are your daughter's "Martha Stewart." Your daughter will want to invite friends into her home precisely because she has grown up watching her mother extend such hospitality to friends and (hopefully) to some strangers.

In our home we had a junk drawer—or you might describe it as a "treat drawer" if you have teens in mind. Our children knew they could always offer their friends access to this drawer. In fact, it was the one drawer that was actually broken in our kitchen, because of its constant use. Though our home was not very large, our children always felt free to invite their friends to come over. Part of their hospitability habit was to point the way to the infamous junk drawer.

> *Do not forget to entertain strangers, for by so doing some people have entertained angels without knowing it* (Hebrews 13:2 NIV).

I certainly don't know whether we have ever entertained angels at the Kendall house, but I can assure you that we have loved many people who have come through our front door. By God's grace, I hope we have loved them well.

Hospitality may seem so simplistic, but there are reasons it is given such prominence in Scripture. Without a doubt it is a little act of kindness that allows for big returns: people feeling loved and attended to.

We love God best when we love each other well.

Diligence and Holy Hugs

Finally, here's another holy habit that is not at all insignificant. A good hug is a gift to the human heart. It doesn't require special training, a college degree, or a bank account. Yet the benefits are priceless.

Does your daughter see you greet others with a holy hug? Has your daughter seen you put your arms around someone who is crying or upset? This gift to the heart requires others-centeredness, especially for those who are not "natural" huggers.

The Kendall family is full of huggers, and at family gatherings we spend so much time hugging each other "Hello" and "Good-bye" that we all need to see a chiropractor after an afternoon together! Any new member of the family actually has to adapt to this hugging ritual.

One of my nieces brought her boyfriend to a Kendall gathering, and the poor guy was totally caught off guard by all the hugging. He later told the story of being hugged "Hello" by some thirty people when he arrived, and the same thirty people hugged their good-byes as he exited. He went on to marry our niece and had us all cracking up at one gathering as he recited his first encounter with the Kendall gang. Hearing his description of our hug-a-thon put us all in hysterics!

Now, I am fully aware that not everyone is the hugging type. But I am going to encourage everyone I can to *learn* to be the hugging type. And the more we model this for our kids, the more naturally it comes to them, even if they go through more awkward, self-conscious years. I am convinced that God is all about hugging! There is a verse that describes those whom God loves as "resting between His shoulders." Sounds like a holy hug to me!

Let the beloved of the LORD rest secure in him, for he shields him all day long, and the one the LORD loves rests between his shoulders (Deuteronomy 33:12 NIV).

Many years ago, two teenage girls knocked on my door. When I opened the door, I recognized one of my daughter's friends, although the other girl was a stranger. I welcomed them both and offered them something to drink. When my daughter's friend introduced the other girl, I heard the name and thought to myself, "This can't be the infamously promiscuous girl from the high school I have heard the kids talk about!"

My daughter's friend said, "Mrs. Kendall I told J_____ that you wrote a book and that you might give her a copy."

I enthusiastically jumped up and got her a copy and signed it to her. When they got ready to leave, of course I gave them both big hugs, and I noticed that this girl held onto me for a few moments.

That night my daughter's friend called and said, "Mrs. Kendall, the moment we got in the car J_____ said, 'I don't remember the last time an adult hugged me!'"

It was a simple hug, but the eternal impact only Jesus knows. He alone who has touched the feelings of our infirmities (see Heb. 4:15) knows how deeply this girl's heart was touched. Later I heard that this promiscuous girl loved my book. My heart's cry was, "Lord Jesus, forgive us for judging promiscuous teens rather than praying for the healing of their starving souls!"

This starvation is what leads them to such flagrant immorality!

> ONLY JESUS KNOWS THE ETERNAL IMPACT OF A SIMPLE HUG.

A holy hug, some encouraging words, an open heart and home, a willingness to serve, and a heart bent toward our Lord in prayer—these are worthy exercises to practice and to build into our daughters' lives. These are the actions *and* the fruits every mom can foster in her Young Lady of Diligence.

Chapter 2: Questions for Discussion

1. Discuss the following quote and compare it to the Scriptures listed:

People who really want to make a difference in the world usually do it, in one way or another. And I've noticed something about people who make a difference in the world: They hold the unshakable conviction that individuals are extremely important, that *every life matters*. They get excited over one smile. They are willing to feed one stomach, educate one mind, and treat one wound. They aren't determined to revolutionize the world all at once; they're satisfied with small changes. Over time, though, the small changes add up. Sometimes they even transform cities and nations, and yes, the world.[5] (See Colossians 3:23-24; First Corinthians 10:31.)

2. Which of the following activities of a Lady of Diligence are holy habits in your life?

   - *Diligence and Internal Jogging*

   - *Diligence and Holy Sweat*

   - *Diligence and Breaking One's Piggy Bank*

   - *Diligence and Hallmark Cards*

   - *Diligence and a Junk Food Drawer*

   - *Diligence and Holy Hugs*

   Share examples of applying these activities to your life and your daughter's.

3. Which of the above activities are not *yet* holy habits in your life?

4. Which of the above activities are presently holy habits being developed in your daughter?

5. Which of the above activities would you most like to see become holy habits in the heart and life of your Young Lady of Diligence?

6. Discuss the reality of being a most important role model in your daughter's life. (See First Corinthians 11:1.)

Raising a Young Lady of Faith

Ruth's Faith

Ruth certainly must have considered the probability of remaining single if she left Moab and went with Naomi. Even though it promised no prospects of a husband, she chose to follow Naomi and Naomi's God back to Bethlehem.

Ruth chose to trust God with her future. She looked not with sensual sight, but through the eyes of faith. She chose to trust with her heart for the future her eyes could not yet see.

God providentially directed Ruth to the field of Boaz. You'll find this divine encounter in chapter 2 of the Book of Ruth. It began when *"...she happened to come to the portion of the field belonging to Boaz..."* (Ruth 2:3).

This leaves no room for manipulation. Ruth's eyes of faith led her to the exact spot where she would meet Mr. Right, Boaz, whose name suggests a pillar of strength.[1] God rewarded Ruth's faith with a husband who lived up to his name.

In Chapter 2 of this book, we looked at some very specific ways for you moms to cultivate diligence in your daughters. Now I want to direct my encouragement toward very practical ways of building the faith of these girls, and hopefully some "big girls" as well.

The old expression about husbands and wives goes: "What's good for the goose is good for the gander." I would make the same claim about mothers and daughters. So I hope that you will take the opportunity to be spurred on in *your* faith walk in this chapter, and particularly through our emphasis on the Word of God: the Bible.

How do we grow in faith? The Bible is filled with teaching about this process; and so it is from God's very Word that we find instruction in raising a Young Lady of Faith. As Paul wrote to the Roman Church in his rich epistle exhorting them: *"So faith comes from hearing, and hearing by the word of Christ"* (Rom. 10:17).

When we study the Bible, we "hear" God's love for us and His instruction to us; we hear about God's character and about the character He would work in us. It is not just any word we are hearing, but the *Word of God* that inspires and nourishes faith. Therefore, the absolute best thing I can focus this chapter on involves how you can set your focus and your daughter's focus on God's Word, the Bible.

Prep Quiz Question No. 5: Does your teen have a No-Bozo Heart Guard? Does she understand the significance of "getting her seven" daily? (See Romans 10:17.)

Getting Her "Seven" Daily

Within mere seconds of asking Jesus to come into my heart and take control of my life, I was given my first Bible. Along with it, the youth leader gave me the most life-impacting advice I have ever had. He said, "Jackie, this is your spiritual food. I want you to read it at least seven minutes each day. Seven minutes reading your Bible will begin to feed your spirit."

As a not-so-sweet sixteen-year-old who had just received God's glorious gift of forgiveness, I was in a very teachable mode. I took the instruction to "get my seven" very seriously, and actually couldn't wait to read my Bible. From that day until this day, I have never "recovered" from this privilege.

I TOOK THE INSTRUCTION TO "GET MY SEVEN" VERY
SERIOUSLY, AND ACTUALLY COULDN'T WAIT TO READ
MY BIBLE. FROM THAT DAY UNTIL THIS DAY, I HAVE
NEVER "RECOVERED" FROM THIS PRIVILEGE.

In addition to the personal privilege of reading and studying the Word of God, it has been the privilege of my life to be called to share the Word with others—not least of all, with my own children. One day this past year my daughter Jessi was running and listening to a podcast by the minister and author Francis Chan. Something he said in this talk caused Jessi to stop still in her tracks, turn off the podcast and call me. She was so excited that I almost missed a few words of her exclamation.

Breathlessly she said, "Mom! I just heard something Francis Chan said and it so reminded me of you that I had to call you this instant!"

My eyes filled with tears as Jessi shared the following quote:

The number one responsibility of every parent is to teach their children to be independently dependent on Jesus and His Word.

If there was one desire I had as a mother, it was this: that my children would become "independently dependent on Jesus and His Word." And as Jessi quoted these words over the phone, it was a true moment of blessing and affirmation—not only because she is a lover of the Word, but because she is raising *her* little daughter with the same intention and hope.

Parents are busily engaged daily in teaching their children so many things, but there is nothing more significant than teaching our children to be dependent upon Jesus and His Word. As a parent I simply made sure that my children knew from a very early age how significant God's Word needed to be in their lives. Reading the Bible and other biblically-sound devotionals began when my children could sit upright. And now my grandbaby, Emma Grace, runs to get her Bible when you tell her it's bedtime—and she's just eighteen months old!

Such passion about God's Word in the lives of those we love is not to be exceptional; it's meant to be the norm. Look at a passage of Scripture that proclaims this truth:

Love the LORD your God with all your heart and with all your soul and with all your strength. These commandments that I give you today are to be upon your hearts. Impress them on your children. Talk about them when you sit at home and when you walk along the road, when you lie down and when you get up (Deuteronomy 6:5-7 NIV).

Do I Need to Repeat Myself?...Yes!

I have always been that mom who was sharing the Word with my kids whether we were on the way to the grocery store or the beach. If the car was full of my kids and their friends, I didn't change my speech to accommodate those who weren't my kids. If I was sharing God's Word with my kids, then the guests were a captive audience.

Sometimes I used to wonder if I was too repetitive, but then a friend of mine who is a Bible scholar sent me an analysis of the word that is translated "impress" in Deuteronomy 6: 7:

Impress them on your children. Talk about them when you sit at home and when you walk along the road, when you lie down and when you get up (NIV).

Here Moses is exhorting the Israelites to teach the commandments of God to their children, or to "impress them" on the children. Let's dig in a bit and see what I learned from the Hebrew as well as the Latin base for our English words.

What my friend laid out for me to see is both the meaning of a word as well as the grammatical tense of the word and how that affects its meaning. First, its meaning. The Hebrew word in this verse is *shanan* and means "to impress upon" or "to teach." Even more accurately, *shanan* could be translated "to inculcate."[2] Now, in English, to inculcate means to "instill (an attitude, habit or idea) by *persistent instruction*"[3] or, in other words, to teach by the same manner repeatedly. This word *inculcate* has a 16th century Latin origin: *inculcat-,* which would translate "pressed in."[4]

Moving from the meaning to the grammar, in the Hebrew, the stem and tense of the word *shanan* is what is called "Piel Perfect." The Piel Stem puts it in the category of an imperative, not only in terms of a command, but of forceful action. The perfect tense of the word in this verse means that the writer meant for the act to be repeated; it is something that has already happened and should continue to happen again and again. In other words, "Keep reminding your children; teach them by repetition." In fact, as my friend pointed out, her professor always said, "All learning is repetition."

Therefore, when it comes to repeating God's Word to our precious children, the process not only *requires* repetition, but God *instructs* parents to teach in that way. So I think we could even call it a "holy repetition," if you will. Moms, please don't worry if you feel you are a little behind. Fear not. Today is a new day, and a perfect day to practice this "Piel Perfect" instruction from the Lord to press the Word into our kids' hearts and begin a "holy repetition!"

A No-Bozo Heart Guard

Here is another kind of holy repetition that can serve our girls as they are growing as Young Ladies of Faith. I spoke at a teen event in Houston and explained to 1400 (mostly junior high) teenage girls the significance of getting their seven minutes of daily Bible reading. I walked back and forth across the stage with my hands in the air, displaying seven fingers and shouting, "Get your seven!"

I exhorted them to be in the Word and grow in faith so that they could outrun the Bozo guys in Houston *and* have a growing faith that would sustain them through all of life's storms. I had no idea what was going to happen with my seven fingers in the air and my shouting, "Get your seven minutes in the Word, girls!"

The girls themselves surprised me when, during the lunch break, a large group of them came running over and were so excited about something they wanted to show me. All of them proceeded to hold up their hands displaying seven fingers, and with the slightest twist of their hands they aligned their thumbs and a double "L" was displayed. Then, like a band of cheerleaders, they all started shouting, "Get your seven and avoid a loser! Get your seven!"

I was so thrilled that I started jumping up and down with them! I had many teen events on my schedule that year, and it would be my joy to tell other teen girls, "Get your seven and avoid a loser!"

Getting your seven in the Word is a great No-Bozo Heart Guard. Why do I believe that? When a girl gets her seven minutes in God's Word, she can't help but grow spiritually. This growth then provokes a desire in her to please the King, thereby making her less attracted to guys who are not growing in their love for the King as she is. This is not a magic formula; this is just an example of *the transforming power of God's Word in the heart of our girls*.

I didn't have a Christian mother or father. I lived in a deeply disturbed home. But my time in God's Word fortified my heart and developed a No-Bozo Heart Guard in the context of family and friends who were not pursuing Jesus.

If your daughter doesn't have this holy habit of getting her seven minutes with God daily, begin to pray and get ready to approach her with this suggestion. Toward the end of this chapter I recommend some methods for your daughter's journey in God's Word. First and foremost, of course, is that you're getting your daily seven, because our children imitate us. Your consistency is an invaluable model. The challenges you are facing in life require strong faith, and faith is inextricably linked to one's daily "face time" with God.

Here's a quote my beloved college mentor shared with me almost forty years ago. It is still true today:

> There is no success, no happiness, and no fulfillment in life apart from a consistent, daily, growing relationship with Jesus through the *Word*.[5]

Parents so want their children to succeed and be happy, but they too often neglect the instruction of the holy repetition of God's Word in the lives of their children. Moms, heed the advice of my college professor who knew that there was no real success in the classroom or life without attention to the Lord and His Word. Without that, your daughter may grow up to pass school, but flunk life.

YOUR CONSISTENCY IS AN INVALUABLE MODEL. THE CHALLENGES YOU ARE FACING IN LIFE REQUIRE STRONG FAITH, AND FAITH IS INEXTRICABLY LINKED TO ONE'S DAILY "FACE TIME" WITH GOD.

Too Busy to "Get Your Seven"

I know you're busy. Of course you are. If you're over twelve, you're busy. Isn't it interesting, though, that we're never too busy to eat? We're never too busy to shop. We're never too busy to watch our favorite shows. We constantly complain about the busyness in our lives and are just too busy to spend time in God's Word.

This is astounding to me, and not because people aren't following a rule to have a quiet time. It's astounding because I have been the beneficiary of receiving comfort and encouragement and wisdom from the Father so regularly from His Word that I can't imagine someone missing out on those blessings!

If you think you are too busy to read the Bible, I promise you, you aren't. I have a friend who likes to blow her hair straight with a diffuser. This takes a bit more time in the morning, and this woman uses that time wisely. She literally opens her Bible and as she is blowing her hair dry and straight, she is turning the pages of her *One Year Bible*.

Here is a great tool for you (no, not the diffuser): many of the women I am close to use the *One Year Bible* as their method for getting their daily seven. I have worked with professional baseball and football players who struggle to make time to read the Bible, and this method has helped many of them be consistent, also.

Why this Bible? Because we are all busy and we are all easily distracted by the daily activities of life. The *One Year Bible* offers a daily format that helps us to be consistent. Every day is divided into four parts: Old Testament, New Testament, Psalms, and Proverbs. These bite-sized increments help us to stay on task; and with four sections, there are four chances to get something meaningful out of our face time with God.

Honestly, if you don't get anything out of the Word, why would you read it? This does not mean that every day brings a profound revelation, but if you are not attentive daily to God's Love Letter, you minimize your chances of being available for His words and His ways of showing love to you.

I am blessed with a large group of friends, and we are all crazy busy. But we are also intentional about keeping our friendships intact. That requires much effort and planning.

You can probably tell the same story. Well, just as you consider the effort of maintaining a great friendship, I hope that you are even more intentional about your relationship with Jesus. Hopefully your friends feel free to *help you* be intentional in your relationship with Him.

Showing your daughter how to have a quiet time is one of the greatest gifts you will ever give her. Recently at a mother-daughter event in West Monroe, Louisiana, I shared about the significance of spending a little time each day reading the Bible. I suggested that the little girls (ages four through nine) go through the devotional *Lady in Waiting for Little Girls.* I also recommended that they look up each verse mentioned in the devotional and mark it with a highlighter. Then they would not only have read the verses, but marked them in *their own* Bibles.

Two days later, a mother sent me a picture of her six-year-old daughter, Nancy Claire, who was in her pajamas, with her blanket and stuffed animal at her side—just the picture of a little one snuggling up before bed. On her lap was an open Bible, and in her hand was a blue highlighter. I just cried when I saw the picture. I was so touched, because I know that Nancy Claire has such an advantage over many millions of little girls who do not have moms who know the significance of a consistent, daily, growing relationship with Jesus and His Word.

Nancy Claire is learning at a young age that *sin will keep you from the Bible, and the Bible will keep you from sin* (see Ps. 119:9,11). Nancy Claire's mom is not a pastor's wife or a missionary or a teacher in a Bible college. Nancy Claire's mom has learned to live in reckless abandon to her Lord, and she makes Jesus look stunning each day in West Monroe, Louisiana.

Mom, the same method that little Nancy Claire learned can be applied to your teen. She can read a copy of *Lady in Waiting* and she can look up each Scripture that is mentioned throughout each chapter—and she can mark these Scriptures in her Bible.

Another fun method of Bible study for a teen is to read through the New Testament (for seven minutes each day), and put a heart in the center of a journal page. Then, inside the heart, she can write the address of the verse that jumped off the page that day. Under the heart, she can write out the verse. This method has helped thousands to slowly hide the Word of God in their own hearts!

Ruth and a Kidnapped Girl—Two Hearts of Faith

As you know, the Book of Ruth is named after its leading lady. This leading lady had a heart of faith that is profoundly displayed in the first chapter of the book. In it, Ruth leaves not only her family and friends but also her hometown to travel to a nation, people, country, and town of strangers who, quite frankly, were not fans of her nationality. Ruth, a Moabite, was leaving hometown security for a new home with Naomi that would require daily faith by Ruth. Her faith ultimately led her to say *no* to the gods of her childhood and *yes* to the one true God.

> *But Ruth said, "Do not urge me to leave you or turn back from following you; for where you go, I will go, and where you lodge, I will lodge. Your people shall be my people, and your God, my God"* (Ruth 1:16).

This choice by Ruth required deep faith. It was the very faith that would lead her to the field where she would meet her Mr. Right and quickly enter her "happily ever after."

Now I will introduce you to another displaced girl whose faith is also an inspiration. Both of these females had hearts of faith that sustained each of them in a new place, a new country, among new people.

Here is the second girl's story. She is one of my heroes. In the fifth chapter of Second Kings, we read about the healing of the leper, Naaman. Most readers focus on the famous commander's healing. Naaman had leprosy and was healed by the prophet after dipping in the Jordan seven times.

> *So he went down and dipped himself seven times in the Jordan, according to the word of the man of God; and his flesh was restored like the flesh of a little child and he was clean* (2 Kings 5:14).

But this miracle was preceded by another miracle often missed by the untrained eye! Let's see if you can spot it:

> *Now Naaman, captain of the army of the king of Aram, was a great man with his master, and highly respected, because by him the Lord*

had given victory to Aram. The man was also a valiant warrior, but he was a leper. Now the Arameans had gone out in bands and had taken captive a little girl from the land of Israel; and she waited on Naaman's wife. She said to her mistress, "I wish that my master were with the prophet who is in Samaria! Then he would cure him of his leprosy." Naaman went in and told his master, saying, "Thus and thus spoke the girl who is from the land of Israel" (2 Kings 5:1-4).

Did you catch the miracle? Did you see the miracle of a young Israelite girl who was kidnapped, taken to a foreign land, and made to be a servant? This girl was not bitter. Did she not miss her family and her hometown? Was she not a victim of heartless kidnapping? *Yes, yes, yes!* But according to what the Scripture tells us about her, this young girl did not let bitterness define her. She did not hold on to unforgiveness like a treasured heirloom. Rather, she professed confidence in the healing God of Israel, and she boldly declared this to her mistress! Somehow this girl had been raised with such a confidence in Jehovah-Rapha (The Lord that Heals), that even in cruel captivity, she could not hide her faith in God.

My grandbaby's storybook Bible expresses this forgiving child's heart perfectly:

> Why would she, of all people, want to help Naaman? Didn't she hate him and want to hurt him back? Didn't she want to make him pay for the wrong he'd done? That is what you would expect, but instead of hating him, she loved him. Instead of hurting him back, she forgave him.[6]

This little girl's parents not only taught her to be independently dependent on God and His truths, but they also taught her how to love by forgiving even what would seem unforgivable.

Have you taught your child to be a good forgiver? Does she have such a growing faith that she is able to bless another person even in difficult circumstances? The nameless, kidnapped girl who helped Naaman had a heart of faith that allowed God to use her not only in the commander's life, but also in the life of the King of Syria (see 2 Kings 5:4-5).

For parents, the holy repetition we discussed is a legacy gift to our girls so their hearts will grow in faith and sustain them in the storms they will encounter. Sadly, we often bequeath our children the inheritance of grudges that they learn to treasure like precious heirlooms; but here in our ancient Scriptures, God gives us a striking example of a child who forgave and blessed.

> A GROWING FAITH DOES NOT IMMUNIZE OUR GIRLS AGAINST PAIN, BUT EQUIPS THEM TO MAKE GOOD CHOICES IN DIFFICULT SITUATIONS.

Whether they encounter the storms of mean girls or Bozo guys, a growing faith does not immunize our girls against pain, but equips them to make good choices in difficult situations—like this kidnapped little girl who did what was right even though she had every reason to withhold goodness from her mistress and master. Although she faced a cruel exit from her parents and hometown, her parents did such a good job teaching her the truths of God's Word that she displayed profound faith and wisdom anyway.

Remember, faith comes by hearing and hearing by God's Word (see Rom. 10:17). This young girl heard enough truth growing up that it sustained her even in captivity.

Obey them completely, and you will display your wisdom and intelligence among the surrounding nations... (Deuteronomy 4:6 NLT).

You Can't Smudge Him Out

Are you already struggling with what you have read so far? Does the training of your daughter seem too daunting a task? Maybe you fear that you have already handicapped your child. Well, here is something I call "hope for Mom on her worst days"—something we can learn from another character in the love story of Ruth, and a woman we've already discussed: Naomi, Ruth's mother-in-law. She described herself in a very interesting manner.

"Don't call me Naomi," she responded. "Instead, call me Mara [bitter] for the Almighty has made life very bitter for me" (Ruth 1:20 NLT).

For more than a decade, I have thought about Naomi and her bitterness. I have thought about the totally understandable bitterness that came as a result of losing her husband and both sons. Yet this bitter woman profoundly impacted the young widow Ruth to choose the God of Israel. I have told so many people that God can use them *even* during their darkest hours when their faith has been outrun by their pain, and bitterness has crept into their hearts! I always quote Naomi's bitter bio which is a reminder that you can't smudge out God's light in you.

> I HAVE TOLD SO MANY PEOPLE THAT GOD CAN USE THEM *EVEN* DURING THEIR DARKEST HOURS WHEN THEIR FAITH HAS BEEN OUTRUN BY THEIR PAIN, AND BITTERNESS HAS CREPT INTO THEIR HEARTS!

Bitter Naomi was still a witness to her widowed daughter-in-law. Ruth chose against the gods of her childhood in Moab and chose the only true God—because of the glimpse of God she got through Naomi.

The treasure of Jesus inside the life of His followers is a presence so powerful and so bright, that even a flawed believer cannot totally extinguish "Jesus the light of the world." Even as I type this, I know someone reading it can think of a person whose "treasure" has been dimmed or diminished by the darkness. I read a quote the other day by Beth Moore that validated this premise I have shared for so many years. It is from her book: *So Long, Insecurity: You've Been a Bad Friend to Us*:

> Nothing brings me more relief than the absolute certainty that human handprints can't smudge the face of God when He's bound and determined to reveal a glimpse of Himself."[7]

When I read that quote I almost did a "hamster dance" of such giddy joy! On our worst days you and I can't smudge out God's revelation of Himself through our lives. When you are irritated, frustrated, and stressed, you can't smudge out the great treasure you contain in your soul. I hope you find some relief from this fact: that we cannot thwart the purposes of God. But more than that, I hope you find *true joy*, the joy of the Lord, in response to His power.

We now have this light shining in our hearts, but we ourselves are like fragile clay jars containing this great treasure. This makes it clear that our great power is from God, not from ourselves (2 Corinthians 4:7 NLT).

This week one of my nieces wrote me an e-mail about the impact of my life on hers. I was amazed by her testimony of the extent of it when, quite honestly, I see her so infrequently. Even rare encounters can produce a long-term impact, because God's intent of revealing Himself can't be smudged out just because our exposures to someone's life are few and far between!

Q.T. KISS Method for You and Your Daughter

Most of us need a simple way to get our "seven" consistently. The Quiet Time KISS Method has worked for me and for many other women. The next few sections include ideas that may be helpful to you and your daughter.

If you already have a consistent time in God's Word, then you can focus on encouraging your daughter to develop this holy habit. If, however, you have allowed your face time with God to disappear from your daily schedule, then today is a great day to restore this holy habit yourself. Whether you need to encourage your daughter or you need the reminder, the following material will hopefully help you both.

A precious young woman, whose mom died when she was fourteen, learned from surrogate moms the significance of daily time in God's Word. She developed the "G.B.T.O" to encourage teen girls to consistently get their "seven." In an e-mail sent to me just before spring break, here is how Courtney Veseay described the G.B.T.O:

What can help you with staying consistent?—G.B.T.O (Girl Behind the Outfit)...just as you lay your clothes out the night before school or your game, etc...also lay out your devotional book and Bible where you are going to be reading the next day, with your clothes...this way you are not only making it easier to get into the Word (PREPARATION), but you are showing God that you are not only concerned with adorning your outward self, but also your HEART![8] (See First Peter 3:3-4.)

Your teen can also keep the "heart record" mentioned earlier, by drawing a heart in the center of her journal page and writing the address of a Scripture that captured her attention. Every time she does this, her heart will grow in faith. She will become a Young Lady of Faith with each encounter with Jesus in the Word.

Jesus Calling

Jesus Calling, a daily devotional by Sarah Young, is a great tool for both moms and daughters. You can look up verses at the bottom of the day's devotion and write out the verse that most speaks to your heart!

Spiritual hunger is different from physical hunger. When you are physically hungry, you eat enough and are full. With spiritual hunger, the more you eat, the more your appetite increases. In a completely paradoxical way, spiritual hunger does not develop through starving—it develops through increased consumption!

Red Circle of Trust

My first college mentor taught me a method of strengthening my faith that I have shared with thousands. She encouraged me to buy a red pencil. What was the red pencil for? I was instructed to start reading through the Book of Psalms and use the red pencil to circle the word *trust* every time I saw it.

So, each day I would read a psalm and be on the hunt for another entry in the "Red Circle of Trust." My college mentor knew that the most important thing she could teach me was to trust God more deeply. She also knew that such deep trust required faith, and faith was not accessed at Target or Nordstrom's. Faith develops through regular time in God's Word.

The simple activity of circling the word *trust* began the healing of a deep heart wound that was only visible to God and those closest to me.

The One Year Bible Method

Face time with God requires intentionality. I have used *The One Year Bible* method of study since 1989. For a hyper, ADHD woman, it has been the easiest for me. The daily reading takes fifteen minutes. For some of my friends, that is still a lot of time. So I have developed the shorter, seven-minute version that I started in 1967 and have discussed throughout this chapter.

Here is the breakdown, using *The One Year Bible*:

- **First year:** Read just the New Testament portions for each day.
- **Second year:** Read just each day's psalm and proverb.
- **Third year:** Read just the Old Testament selection for each day.

This small increment of Bible reading time allows for any journaling or for writing out a key verse in a journal. And here is my most simple key to journaling: *just write something!* Remember, Mom, this is the KISS method (Keep It Simple Stupid or, for your young ones, Keep It Simple Silly). The busiest woman I know uses this method, and she has become quite the Bible scholar in the decade since she implemented it.

> HERE IS MY MOST SIMPLE KEY TO JOURNALING: *JUST WRITE SOMETHING!*

Incomparable Benefit of Bible Reading— Growing Faith

As a mom, a growing faith is a must; but clearly your daughter has the same need. A growing faith will help her resist dating Bozo guys who don't love Jesus (see Josh. 23:12-13). A growing faith will sustain her when her BFF is not speaking to her and on those Friday nights when she isn't invited to the party where other kids are making poor choices.

It will help her when you say "No" to her dating before she turns sixteen (which I discuss in Chapter Seven). And even when she can date, a growing faith will enable her to endure another dateless Friday night when there is no one to hang out with but Mom and Dad (my own daughter lived through this trauma).

A growing faith will encourage your daughter when she feels like she has no friends. If she goes to college or into the work force and is stunned that she is *still* not dating, a growing faith will hold her up. Likewise, if her dream of a "MRS. Degree" is not attained in college, this faith will steady her heart. This growing faith will fortify her patience to wait for a godly guy to befriend and date and eventually marry.

There is so much more—everything in life—that faith guides us through and supports us in. If I focus on a young woman's relational life here, it is not because her education or career or ministry experiences do not also require the undergirding of her growing faith, it is because *time and time again* throughout forty years of ministry, the primary story I hear is of girls becoming shipwrecked in the storms of relationships. They are hit and almost sunk by the challenges and expectations in this realm. So I want them to grow in their sustaining faith in all things, but I emphasize this area here for moms to *start early*. Just because a girl is too young to date, doesn't mean it's too early to train her heart toward the Lover of her Soul.

> JUST BECAUSE A GIRL IS TOO YOUNG TO DATE, DOESN'T MEAN IT'S TOO EARLY TO TRAIN HER HEART TOWARD THE LOVER OF HER SOUL.

Like our heroine Ruth, you and your daughter can make a difference in this world through the daily growing of your faith in our incomparable God. Consider putting the following verse on a Post-It Note and sticking it on your bathroom mirror. Of all the verses in the Bible, it was *this* verse that I framed and gave to my friends as a party favor at a "milestone" birthday celebration!

O Lord, You are my God; I will exalt you and praise your name, for in perfect faithfulness you have done marvelous things, things planned long ago (Isaiah 25:1 NIV).

Chapter 3: Questions for Discussion

1. Did you know that Bible study and strong faith are inextricably linked? (See Romans 10:17.)

2. Does your daughter know how to comfort a friend with God's Word, as Libby comforted Maddie? (See Chapter 2.)

3. Who is the Ultimate Tutor during quiet time? (See James 1:5.)

4. Who needs a daily quiet time?

   a. Powerful people, such as kings (see Deut. 17:18-19).

   b. "Beautiful people," such as celebrities (see Amos 8:11-13).

   c. All people desiring to be true followers of Christ (see John 8:31).

5. What is available daily in God's Word? (Examine this sampler from Psalms 119.)

   a. Wonderful truths (see verse 18)

   b. Wise advice (see verse 24)

   c. Encouragement for the discouraged (see verse 25)

   d. Hope for those in grief and despair (see verse 28)

   e. Discernment between worthy and worthless things (see verse 37)

   f. Wisdom beyond one's years (see verses 99-100)

   g. Insight to spot false belief systems (see verses 104,130)

   h. Rest and peace for the weary soul (see verse 165)

6. "A Bible that is falling apart belongs to someone whose life isn't." Discuss this phrase.

7. Why is it a struggle for you to have daily quiet time?

8. What devotional method has worked the best for you? Share it with your group.

Recommendations for Discussion

1. Practical preparation for your quiet time:

a. The same chair

b. The same Bible

c. The same journal (journal in composition book, journal book, or the Bible margins)

d. A notepad

e. The same pen

f. Study helps nearby—ESV Study Bible for the hard questions

CHAPTER 4

Raising a Young Lady of Virtue

Ruth's Virtue

One of life's most costly and beautiful objects is born out of pain and irritation—the pearl. The pearl begins as a mere grain of sand in the belly of an oyster that then secretes layers of a substance to protect itself from the agitation of the foreign particle.

Like the oyster, Ruth experienced many irritations and trials in her young life. She grieved the deaths of her father-in-law, brother-in-law, and husband. She bravely faced the turmoil of a radically altered direction in her life as well as a move to a foreign land with a bitter mother-in-law. When she arrived in that strange land, the trials did not end. She was immediately thrown into a new working situation among total strangers with new customs. Through all this stress, her new faith began to wrap itself around the painful situations. The by-product was a pearl.

What was it that enabled Ruth to catch Boaz's attention? Was it her gorgeous hair or beautiful eyes? No! The answer is found in Boaz's response to her question in Ruth, chapter 2.

Then she fell on her face, bowing to the ground and said to him, "Why have I found favor in your sight that you should take notice of me, since I am a foreigner?" And Boaz answered and said to her, "All that you have done for your mother-in-law after the death of your husband has been fully reported to me, and how you left your father and your mother and the land of your birth, and came to a people that you did not previously know" (Ruth 2:10-11).

Boaz was attracted to the pearl of Ruth's virtue and character displayed in her life. A woman of virtue is irresistible to a godly man. It is a pearl worth pursuing.

> A WOMAN OF VIRTUE IS IRRESISTIBLE TO A GODLY MAN. VIRTUE IS A PEARL WORTH PURSUING.

Is Virtue Extinct in the 21st Century?

In the 21st century, the word *virtue* is not a regular guest in the mainstream vocabulary or colloquial speech. Virtue is probably perceived as a word for the Puritan period of American history and totally out of date today. One of the primary definitions of the word *virtue* is "moral excellence."[1] I know our society is all about "excellence" but it has tried to divorce itself from the *moral* aspect of any excellence.

The leading man in the Book of Ruth was drawn to the leading lady because of the obvious virtue displayed in her life through her choices. In modern times like these, virtue is not what most guys are concerned about; they are often too busy looking at the exterior and are not even concerned about the interior. And certainly a Bozo is more concerned about a girl's "headlights" and "taillights" than the moral excellence of her heart.

During the last few years, I've been getting the impression that my ideals are becoming so outdated that very few will be listening anymore to my ranting and raving about girls flashing their headlights and taillights. In fact, a young rookie playing for the Atlanta Braves told his chaplain, "I want to look upon women in purity but they keep flashing their headlights and taillights—making it almost impossible to look at a woman and not lust!"

This young baseball player wants to live honorably, but, honestly, he needs help from us women and—take note Mom—even the girls.

I have made a covenant with my eyes not to look lustfully at a girl (Job 31:1 NIV).

No wonder God described Job as a blameless man. A man who can resist lusting after local "eye candy" is indeed a noble creature. Job was a Boaz ahead of his time. Recently I saw a post on Facebook written by a young woman venting about ideals that are sorely not understood by most teenagers.

Her ranting reminded me of all the principles that I am trying to teach teens and college students. It was so much fun to look up this young woman, see her *youth,* and realize that we are on the same page. Three decades separate us, yet we are shouting the same truths from the mountaintops! Here is a glimpse of what this young woman posted on her blog:

...If you choose to wear shirts that show off your breasts, you will attract boys. To be more specific, you will attract the kind of boys that like to look down girls' shirts. If you want to date a guy who likes to look at other girls' breasts and chase skirts, then great job; keep it up. *If you don't* want to date a guy who ogles at the breasts of other women, then maybe you should stop offering your own breasts up for the ogling. All attention is not equal. You think you want attention, but you don't. You want respect. All attention is not equal....

Don't play coy or stupid or helpless to get attention. Don't pretend something is too heavy so that a boy will carry it for you. Don't play dumb to stroke someone's ego. Don't bat your eyelashes in exchange for attention and expect to be taken seriously, ever. You can't have it both ways. Either you show the world that you have a brain and passions and skills, or you don't. There are no damsels in distress managing corporations, running countries, or managing households. The minute you start batting eyelashes, eyelashes is all you've got....

You are beautiful. You are enough. The world we live in is twisted and broken, and for your entire life you will be subjected to all kinds of lies that tell you that you are not enough. You are not thin enough. You are not tan enough. You are not smooth, soft, shiny, firm, tight, fit, silky, blonde, hairless enough. Your teeth are not white enough. Your legs are not long enough. Your clothes are not stylish enough. You are not educated enough. You don't have enough experience. You are not creative enough.

There is a beauty industry, a fashion industry, a television industry, (and most unfortunately) a pornography industry: and all of these have unique ways of communicating to bright young women: you are not beautiful, sexy, smart or valuable enough....

You are beautiful. You are valuable. You are enough.[2]

> "THE MINUTE YOU START BATTING EYELASHES, EYELASHES [ARE] ALL YOU'VE GOT."

You Are More Than Your Breast Size

I so appreciate what our blogger, Kate, said to those who would have the courage to read her bold remarks. Kate is keenly aware that girls are too often mere sex objects or eye candy. Then they are exploited and tossed away for a new model.

I was in the Dallas airport waiting for my luggage when I saw a mother and daughter walk up to the luggage carousel. The daughter was not dressed modestly. She was not a display of virtue. What was so sad is that the girl was probably barely a teenager and already was eye candy for some man's lustful appetite. What was so devastating to me was watching older men just staring at this young child while mom was busy getting their luggage! I wanted to walk over and throw a cup of cold water in the face of the mom. I wanted to wake her up from her sleep, morally speaking, and tell her that her daughter is being ogled by several dirty old men! I wanted to ask her frankly, "Are you proud of yourself, Mom?"

Most moms are absolutely clueless to what they are grooming their daughters to be. Moms think they are just letting their daughters dress like the current trend! Most Christian households in America could use a "revival" in their closets. Several years ago, one of my daughter's friends read the book *Every Man's Battle*, and she was so convicted that she went home and cleaned her closet. She got rid of any outfit that would cause the guys in her life to "lust rather than respect her." Her closet had a renovation and consecration because of the heart that had been convicted of trendy compromise.

Recently my new daughter-in-law posted on Facebook:

Excuse me. Your dress should be tight enough to show you're a woman but lose enough to show you're a lady. Thank you.

Help With Modesty for Moms

Does your daughter have a consecrated closet? Does she dress modestly, or is she eye candy for the boys as well as the men around her? These are such hard questions to ask, but ladies, I live in South Florida and what I see at the mall and even at church—much of it looks like it belongs on a beach.

Recently my pastor gave the best explanation of what it is to dress modestly. Dr. Scroggins said, "Modesty is presenting yourself so that the attention of other people is drawn to your face."

Here's the simple question to ask: what does my outfit draw attention to? Does my outfit enhance my modesty or challenge its existence?

> HERE'S THE SIMPLE QUESTION TO ASK: DOES YOUR OUTFIT ENHANCE YOUR MODESTY OR CHALLENGE ITS EXISTENCE?

If your daughter wants to purchase something that would not be defined as modest, then you simply say, "Sweetheart, I love you too much to let you wear such an outfit."

I recently saw an article in *The Wall Street Journal* that discussed the lack of "modest" dresses available for purchase for prom night. The article had several photos of the current available prom dresses, and I couldn't help but think a girl might as well go to Victoria's Secret, purchase lingerie, and wear *that* to the prom.[3]

Ironically, speaking of the famous lingerie store, the media paid some notable attention to a Victoria's Secret model who, as a result of reading the Bible, made a decision to actually discontinue modeling lingerie. By being a Lady of Faith and studying God's Word, she discovered the contradiction of being a follower of Jesus and modeling lingerie:

> Kylie Bisutti, winner of the 2009 Victoria's Secret Model Search, on why she gave up lingerie modeling. Bisutti continues to model clothing. "My body should only be for my husband. I'm a Christian," she told Fox News, "and reading the Bible more, I was becoming convicted of it."[4]

It is likely that few of us would lose the kind of money and attention that this young lady has committed to by virtue of this decision. In her industry, this choice is practically a career killer! Like Ruth, who took the "high road" by following Naomi to Israel, Kylie Bisutti took the high road of virtue by risking her career for the right, moral choice.

Modesty and Little Girls

Now, your daughter might be years away from prom night, but dressing modestly is as *critical* an issue in elementary schools as in junior high schools. Virtue and modesty are not just teen issues!

Recently a leader in a Christian school had to discipline several elementary girls for taking pictures in their underwear and sending them to boys on campus. The next week this Christian school leader had to discipline an elementary girl for passing a note in Bible class in which she mentioned wanting to do something to a boy's private area! This Christian school leader said that in all her years of leadership she had never seen such bold, defiant sexual behavior from little girls. I wanted to scream and cry at the same time when I heard the story. Where are the mothers who are responsible for raising these girls to be Ladies of Virtue? Why aren't they raising them to be Proverbs 31 women rather than Proverbs 6:20-35 women?

Our daughters should have wardrobes reflective, not of Hollywood, but of their being owned by a most holy God!

Do you not know that your body is a temple of the Holy Spirit who is in you, whom you have from God, and that you are not your own? For you have been bought with a price: therefore glorify God in your body (1 Corinthians 6:19-20).

Mom, one of the most basic principles for keeping your daughter from being Bozo bait, is to lovingly monitor her clothing. Modesty is not alluring to a Bozo.

VIRTUE AND MODESTY ARE NOT JUST TEEN ISSUES!

Who Do Young Ladies of Virtue Date?

And now, another principle to protect your daughter from being Bozo bait: the Biblical command for a Christian girl to date only guys who encourage her spiritually.

One of the earliest principles I learned as a new Christian was that I shouldn't date non-Christians. I was at a huge youth leadership retreat at Westmont College in Santa Barbara when I first heard a teaching on not dating nonbelievers. When the teacher read Second Corinthians 6:14, I knew immediately that I needed to break up with my boyfriend when I returned home. I was not from a Christian home, so no one in my family understood why I broke up with him. When I tried to explain, they all shook their heads in disapproval of my decision.

Do not be yoked together with unbelievers. For what do righteousness and wickedness have in common? Or what fellowship can light have with darkness? (2 Corinthians 6:14 NIV)

What has troubled me over the last four decades is how casually Christians handle the topic of Christians dating non-Christians. Too often a young girl will say to me, "Well Mrs. Kendall, I've only had one date with him."

I immediately reply, "Every date is a potential mate. Nobody marries somebody they didn't date. So why would you date someone who doesn't love Jesus? Why find yourself getting caught up and attracted to someone who might seduce you away from the ultimate reason you're on this planet—to bring Jesus glory?"

Prep Quiz Question No. 16: Does your teen know how to avoid wearing chains on her wedding day?

Years ago I wrote about a bride coming down the aisle dressed in a beautiful wedding gown that was covered in chains and wrapped in a whip. This word picture was based on a passage of Scripture:

> *But if you turn away and ally yourselves with the survivors of these nations that remain among you and if you intermarry with them and associate with them, then you may be sure that the LORD your God will no longer drive out these nations before you. Instead, they will become snares and traps for you, whips on your backs and thorns in your eyes...* (Joshua 23:12-13 NIV).

Toothpicks in Eyeballs

What a gory topic! What could I possibly be referring to? The topic refers to the pain people inflict upon themselves when they disobey the ancient principle presented in the preceding verses of Joshua 23:12-13.

As I mentioned above, when I was a new Christian, I was taught this ancient principle by one of my spiritual mentors. The principle was simple: Do not date nonbelievers. I have given this same counsel to many teenage girls and single women throughout the last two decades. This counsel is not from a backwoods, legalistic mentality; it is one of the oldest principles for a "holy race" (see Ezra 9:2).

Even though this principle is clearly stated in both the Old and New Testaments, I continue to meet women (young and not so young) who think it is a rule created merely by the religion of man, and not a principle instituted by a loving heavenly Father. I know so many unhappy women who are married to nonbelievers. Time and time again, they admit that they had disregarded this biblical principle when they were dating. In disregarding the principle, these women inflicted whips, snares, and thorns on themselves—a masochistic behavior. When a person knowingly disregards any biblical injunction, it will result in self-injury. God's principles are for our protection, but it takes faith to believe that God is not a killjoy.

I always ask women who are married to nonbelievers if anyone warned them about their choices to date and eventually marry these men. Often they say, "No one challenged me or even warned me about dating a man who didn't know Jesus personally."

I am concerned that those of us who know the Lord intimately would have the courage of a Micaiah (see 2 Chron. 18). Micaiah would tell the truth even if the person ended up hating him for what he said. We need courage to speak the truth to any teenage girl or single woman who is considering dating a nonbeliever. We should warn her about the inevitable pain of "toothpicks in her eyes." I would rather make a gal miserable for a little while by being honest than to have her spend years in a miserable marriage because I didn't have a "Micaiah spirit" when it came to telling the truth.

> I WOULD RATHER MAKE A GAL MISERABLE FOR A LITTLE WHILE BY BEING HONEST THAN TO HAVE HER SPEND YEARS IN A MISERABLE MARRIAGE BECAUSE I DIDN'T HAVE A "MICAIAH SPIRIT" WHEN IT CAME TO TELLING THE TRUTH.

We cannot keep women or young ladies from disobeying God, but we can at least warn them about such masochistic behaviors on their part. We need to warn them as the apostle Paul did: *"Do not be yoked together with unbelievers"* (2 Cor. 6:14a NIV).

I would remind you, Mom, that dating is not simply a social activity. Who your daughter wants to date is a reflection of her depth, spiritually speaking. You need to pay attention to which boys your daughter is crushing on, because it reveals her heart.

*They took their daughters to be their wives, and gave their daughters to their sons, and **served their gods*** (Judges 3:6 KJV).

Every date is a potential mate, and one's mate is one of God's most powerful sanctifying tools. We want the best for our daughters and *God's* best is the key. So let's not underplay the significance of what these choices reveal.

Greatest Self-Deception—Missionary Dating

A common self-deception among girls as well as women is the power that the girl thinks she has to *change* the one she has a crush on, admires from afar, or has begun to date. I have spoken with thousands of girls who have tried to explain to me their reasoning that justifies dating nonbelievers. I have even had parents explain what "nice" guys their daughters are dating. I always ask, "Is he a Christian?"

Most parents respond defensively, "I don't know, but he comes from a good family."

When I follow up with the second question: "What do you mean by a good family?" I unfortunately find that, more often than not, *good* means *rich*. Since the first woman ate from the forbidden tree, women have assumed that they are smarter than God and have the power to change those who become the "objects" of their desire.

> SINCE THE FIRST WOMAN ATE FROM THE FORBIDDEN TREE, WOMEN HAVE ASSUMED THAT THEY ARE SMARTER THAN GOD AND HAVE THE POWER TO CHANGE THOSE WHO BECOME THE "OBJECTS" OF THEIR DESIRE.

Here is a classic example of how early this propensity takes root in a girl's heart. Teenagers have told me that it is OK for them to date nonbelievers because their parents weren't believers when they got married and now they are followers of Jesus.

I immediately share a clarifying reality: these people were *blind* when they were married, and coming to Jesus was a *mercy* gift. But I explain to the girl that she is not blind; she is disobeying a clear command as a follower of Jesus. Therefore, she can't assume she will get that mercy. Yet, she can count on being disciplined by God for disobeying the principle of being "unequally attached to a nonbeliever."

Encourage your precious daughter to resist the fantasy of trying to outsmart God.

There is no wisdom, no insight, no plan that can succeed against the LORD (Proverbs 21:30 NIV).

Even Ninth-Grade Boys Know This

My sister-in-law, DeDe, shared a fascinating experience with me about teaching ninth-graders some of the principles from *Lady in Waiting*. The class was composed of both guys and girls. She passed out the following list and asked the students to follow the directions at the top:

Put a check beside each of the following characteristics you can change in your husband after marriage:

1. Unwillingness to communicate

2. Dominating ego

3. Bad temper

4. Argumentative tendencies

5. Difficulty in apologizing

6. Bad language

7. Unwillingness to be in involved with church

8. Inability to keep a job

9. Jealousy

10. Self-centeredness

11. Depression

12. Unwillingness to give

13. Wandering eyes

14. Lying

15. Immaturity

16. Workaholic tendencies

DeDe watched in absolute amazement as the girls busily checked several of the items on the list above. Ninth-grade girls were already displaying the self-deception of thinking one human being can change another. After seeing all the checked items on the girls' lists, she noticed that the boys had not checked *any* items on their lists. When asked why they didn't check anything, several boys spoke up saying, "I can't change another person's behavior."

Here we have ninth-grade boys who knew they couldn't change a girl, much less a wife someday. The girls in the class were surprised at the boys' comments and began to argue about a person's capacity to change "the object of their love." DeDe started laughing as she listened to the girls defend their power to change someone, and the boys' response: "No way!"

How amazing that even ninth-grade boys are able to grasp this reality when grown women labor in vain to try and change their Bozo men into classic Boazes!

HOW AMAZING THAT EVEN NINTH-GRADE BOYS REALIZE THAT YOU CANNOT CHANGE ANOTHER HUMAN BEING, WHEN GROWN WOMEN LABOR IN VAIN TO TRY AND CHANGE THEIR BOZO MEN INTO CLASSIC BOAZES!

Women of all ages and stages of life constantly search for the means to change the men they love. Yet, simultaneously, there are support groups full of people who have reached the ends of their ropes in attempting to do so, and who gather across the United States to discuss the foolishness of the endeavor.

This is not to say that we cannot inspire one another; but let me be crystal clear: only God can change a person's interior.

Pray for a "Tigger" in Your Daughter's Life

When our daughter Jessi entered seventh grade, she joined the track team. She had run in elementary school but now she was in junior high and the training was a little more demanding. There was an older girl who our daughter would constantly speak about; this girl always encouraged Jessi when she ran. The girl was endearingly called "Tigger." Her name was Alicia Tager, hence the nickname. We met this encouraging girl at the track meets, and she was a delight to speak to, even for a moment.

One day our daughter mentioned that Tigger wanted to pick her up early and drive her to school where they could have a short Bible study together. This precious high school girl began picking up our daughter each week. They would then go to the school gym where they would share what they had been reading that week in their Bibles.

As a parent, I had already spent years encouraging Jessi to read her Bible and journal some of her findings; but Tigger's encouragement took Jessi to an even deeper level—peer to peer! Even after Tigger graduated from high school, she continued to encourage our daughter spiritually.

Does your daughter have a Tigger in her life? If not, start asking Jesus for such an influence. Raising a Young Lady of Virtue requires all the godly help He sends us. Also Mom, pray about the influence you can have on your children's friends. It was a real delight when Tigger, who was such an encourager, started to call me "Mrs. Claus" because I was always encouraging so many children.

This precious girl did not come from a Christian home. One of her friends from school reached out to her, and the friend's family influenced her to walk more closely with the Lord. So, one family encouraged Tigger and then Tigger encouraged our girl. I then had the privilege of cheering on Tigger after she graduated from college and went on to seminary. She married a pastor and serves with her husband in their church which is twenty minutes away from where our daughter, Jessi, and her pastor husband serve. After all these years, these young women continue to "run the race" on God's team of willing encouragers.

Moms, just as you want to pay attention to the boys your daughter pays attention to, so you want to be aware of the friends she surrounds herself with. Parents teach virtue, but friends enhance or tarnish virtue. As our daughters associate, they *become*. Their closest friends are a glimpse of their future.

Do not be misled: "Bad company corrupts good character" (1 Corinthians 15:33 NIV).

Does your daughter see you with friends who obviously propel you closer to God? Or does your daughter see you socializing with women who are spiritually mediocre and do not encourage your walk with Jesus? Do you have friends in your life who are like Daniel's friends?

> ## PARENTS TEACH VIRTUE, BUT FRIENDS ENHANCE OR TARNISH VIRTUE.

I remember thinking about Daniel, who was called *"a man greatly beloved"* of God (Dan. 10:11 KJV). In the Hebrew, the word translated "beloved" means not only "great delight" and "great desire," but also "delectable."[5]

Wow, Daniel's life was actually delectable to God. What amazing favor. Tears filled my eyes as I thought about Daniel, because my heart yearns for my own life to be delectable to God.

As I looked more closely at Daniel's life, I read about his three friends, and the Lord showed me something truly exciting. We know Daniel's friends as Shadrach, Meshach, and Abednego, the names they were given in captivity in Babylon. Their not-so-famous Hebrew names were Hananiah, Mishael, and Azariah. As I studied the Hebrew translations and meanings of these names, I discovered what kind of friends Daniel had. They are the kind we all need: friends who passionately want to follow Jesus.

- Hananiah means: The Lord is gracious.[6]

- Mishael means: Who is like our God?[7]

- Azariah means: The Lord is my help.[8]

Just imagine! Their very names held the messages those friends needed to give one another when all three were cast into the fiery furnace (see Dan. 3). Their names described the gracious, incomparable, helping God who showed up in the furnace as the fourth man. The Lord, who walked through the fire with them, was the embodiment of all three of their names!

Do you have friends who remind you that the Lord is gracious (Jehovah-raah), that He is our helper (El Shaddai), and that He is an incomparable God (El Elyon)? As we associate with others, we become a reflection of those with whom we spend time (see Amos 3:3; Prov. 13:20).

Does your life reflect that you have the gift of friends like Daniel? Hananiah, Mishael, and Azariah had their names changed by the Babylonian captors, but their captors couldn't change their hearts. Their hearts remained passionately committed to their incomparable God.

Mom, start asking God daily for friends like Daniel and a special friend like "Tigger" to come into your daughter's life and cheer on her virtue and love for Jesus. Do you have such friends? If not, by all means pray for godly friends to come your way, as well!

Chapter 4—Questions for Discussion

1. Is virtue extinct in the 21st century? Read Jeremiah 6:16 and Amos 8:11-14.

2. "Modesty is presenting yourself so that the attention of other people is drawn to your face." Discuss this quote. (See Job 31:1.)

3. Does your daughter's closet need some consecration? (See First Corinthians 6:19-20.)

4. Does your daughter already know about not dating non-Christians? (See Second Corinthians 6:14 and Joshua 23:12-13.) Did you marry a nonbeliever?

5. Discuss your propensity to try and change others. Discuss what the ninth-grade boys knew about not being able to change others.

6. Can you think of three women in your life who encourage you as Daniel's friends encouraged him? (See Amos 3:3 and Proverbs 13:20.)

7. Does your daughter have a "Tigger" in her life? (See Hebrews 10:24.)

8. Can you name even one girl in your daughter's life who encourages her spiritually?

9. Enhanced reminder: Virtue is who you are when no one is looking. Examine the following Virtues Checklist (not exhaustive, but a good start):

   a. Courage (see Josh. 1:6-8)

   b. Honesty (see Isa. 33:15; Ps.15:2)

   c. Respect (see Prov. 9:10; Eph. 6:5-9)

   d. Generosity (see Prov. 11:24)

   e. Compassion (see Eph. 4:32; 1 Pet. 3:8)

   f. Patience (see Ps. 37:7-9)

   g. Perseverance (see Rom. 5:3-5)

   h. Loyalty (see Prov. 17:17)

   i. Forgiving (Matt. 18:21-22)

CHAPTER 5

Raising a Young Lady of Devotion

Ruth's Devotion

Boaz spoke of Ruth's devotion to God when he said:

May the LORD reward your work, and your wages be full from the LORD, the God of Israel, under whose wings you have come to seek refuge (Ruth 2:12).

Ruth chose to cling to her mother-in-law's God as her own, even though Naomi had drawn a negative, harsh picture of Him. She said to them:

Do not call me Naomi; call me Mara, for the Almighty has dealt very bitterly with me. I went out full, but the LORD as brought me back empty. Why do you call me Naomi, since the LORD has witnessed against me and the Almighty has afflicted me?" (Ruth 1:20-21)

Who would choose to be devoted to a God characterized like Naomi's? Though Ruth clung to her as a mother, she did *not* accept Naomi's view of God for herself.

If we think of Him [God] as cold and exacting, we shall find it impossible to love Him, and our lives will be ridden with servile fear.[1]

I love words and I love to dig in and learn their deepest meaning. Here, in this chapter, we will look at some of what *devotion* to God looks like, and a lot of what it does not look like. To begin with, however, it is helpful to understand a distinction between devotion and faith. They function hand in hand, to be sure, but very simply put, devotion is the acting out of our faith. The Latin word from which we derive "devote" means to consecrate by a vow or to act with loyalty and fidelity. Therefore, if our heart and mind's posture before God is faith in Him, our right actions stemming from that faith are the actions of devotion.

Modeling Hope or Hopelessness

Certainly your life, like Naomi and Ruth's, has gone through seasons of great challenge and seemingly relentless trial. While devotion to God is an *every*day virtue, our responsiveness to Him in tough times is a critical indicator of our faith. Does your daughter see you modeling hope more often than hopelessness? Would she describe you more like Ruth, devoted to God even in difficult circumstances or more like Naomi, who wanted to be called "Mara," because she was embittered by her circumstances?

Our devotion to God is primarily about our relationship with *Him*, and certainly our passion for Him, but those we love are watching that devotion as it ebbs and flows through our lives each day.

While being driven to my hotel after finishing a mother-daughter event, I turned on my phone and discovered I had a long text from our daughter, Jessi. This is one of the most precious gifts ever given to my heart.

> I just have to thank you from the deepest part of my heart for your relentless pursuit of Jesus and zeal for His Word. You have never allowed your life season, responsibilities, hard or easy circumstances to dictate or come before your seeking Jesus first. I just want to make sure you always know how much you have and still do impact me more than any other woman I know.

This text reminded me that no matter what I have gone through—trials galore or deliriously joyful blessings—my devotion to God has remained consistent. And for that, I marvel as much as anyone, since the very capacity to be consistent is a gift of the Holy Spirit.

The modeling of our devotion to God continues to impact our daughters even when they have left home, gotten married, and become mothers themselves. Coincidentally, Jessi sent this text to me four days before she and her hubby, Drew, surprised Ken and me with the wonderful news that we would finally be grandparents! Less than a year later, sitting with Jessi as she held her new baby in her arms, she expressed her concern that she could start neglecting her quiet time with Jesus because of sheer exhaustion. What a precious gift to hear her concern and to witness her commitment to persevere.

Mom—modeling devotion to the Lord that continues to the next generation is truly an unfathomable privilege!

Unfathomable Impact of a Devoted Mom

Recently, while reading Eric Metaxas' massive biography of Dietrich Bonhoeffer *(Bonhoeffer: Pastor, Martyr, Prophet, Spy)*, I came across such inspiring information that I had to stop reading and include my findings in this chapter. Bonhoeffer's own book, *The Cost of Discipleship*, had profoundly impacted me as a young follower of Jesus. His writing helped me realize that salvation was free, but discipleship would cost me everything.

Now, reading the highly acclaimed biography by Eric Metaxas (though 577 pages long), was something I had wanted to do for almost a year. Reading about Bonhoeffer's upbringing, I found myself particularly interested in the people who shaped this amazing man of God. Here is a paragraph from the very first chapter of the book:

"Karl Bonhoeffer [Dietrich's father] would not have called himself a Christian, but he respected his wife's tutelage of the children....She was the granddaughter, daughter, and sister of men whose lives were given to theology, and he knew she was serious about her faith and had hired governesses who were serious about it. He was present at family religious activities and at the holiday celebrations his wife orchestrated, which invariably included hymns, Bible readings, and prayers....It was an excellent environment for the budding theologian [Dietrich] in their midst...."There was no place for false piety or any kind of bogus religiosity in our home," [Dietrich's sibling] said....Mere church going held little charm for her. The concept of cheap grace that Dietrich would later make so famous might have had its origins in his mother, perhaps not the term, but the idea behind it, that faith without works is not faith at all...."[2]

I have met so many mothers concerned about having to be the spiritual leaders in their homes because of the lack of a husband's involvement. I compassionately hear their concern; yet I also know too many wonderful followers of Jesus who, like Dietrich Bonhoeffer, were more profoundly impacted by the spiritual lives of their mothers than their fathers.

Of course we want our husbands to join us in the mentoring and impacting of our children for the glory of God. The Word of God has given this assignment to men and women alike (see Deut. 6:7-9). You and I will someday give an accounting for the spiritual influence we had not only on our children but also all the other children who came into our lives through our children. Don't let your husband's lack of devotion distract you from your privilege to model a daily devotion to Jesus before your children *and* your husband (see Pet. 3:1).

> YOU AND I WILL SOMEDAY GIVE AN ACCOUNTING FOR THE SPIRITUAL INFLUENCE WE HAD NOT ONLY ON OUR CHILDREN BUT ALSO ALL THE OTHER CHILDREN WHO CAME INTO OUR LIVES THROUGH OUR CHILDREN.

Mission Fields at the Front Door

You, as a mom, are one of God's greatest secret weapons! He knows how strategically you have been placed in your sphere of influence. Each friend whom your child attracts into that sphere is a mission field for you. As a mom, you get to imprint on the hearts and minds of these kids the image of someone who loves people to Christ (see 2 Cor. 5:17-20). Like my kids would say, "Mom, that is a no brainer."

My husband and I took a college student named Crystal to lunch after church (something we try to do as often as possible). We asked her to share with us her testimony of coming to know Jesus intimately. Her immediate reply penetrated my heart; I wanted to post it on the hearts of all the moms

I know. Crystal said, "I came to *know* the Lord at a youth camp, but I came to *love* the Lord through the Jacob family."

You and I have the privilege of encouraging young women in their devotion to God, not only our daughters, but the girls our daughters bring home.

I have written about this in earlier chapters, but it bears repeating: your children will attract a variety of young people who might end up in your living room. When the mission field comes through your door, you may be tempted to say, "Oh no, I don't like that boy or girl."

Reflect before you respond. *Pray* before you react. Be careful not to reject the child quickly, because he or she has been delivered to your family room by the Holy One. Your first response may be, "Not this type of child, Lord! Isn't it time for her to go home?"

You cannot love your kids' friends to Jesus without accepting them where they are and praying for where they need to go. When you and I learn to do both, we will effectively fulfill our place in this mission field that God delivered to us.

> REFLECT BEFORE YOU RESPOND. *PRAY* BEFORE YOU REACT. BE CAREFUL NOT TO REJECT A CHILD QUICKLY, BECAUSE HE OR SHE HAS BEEN DELIVERED TO YOUR FAMILY ROOM BY THE HOLY ONE.

The precious strangers who come through your front door need a glimpse of a Lady of Devotion—and hopefully a mother-daughter demo of devotion to God! When our kids were in junior high and high school, I may have looked pretty foolish as I loved on kids who were less than perfect. In fact, I know that some of the teens thought I was absolutely clueless about their poor choices. These teens would assume I didn't know the truth about them, because I so loved them. As the teenagers came to learn about how much I actually knew, they were stunned that I treated them so lovingly. As a follower of Jesus whom they *could see,* I knew that, unless I loved them, they would have a difficult time believing they were loved by the God they *couldn't see.*

If we don't love people, they'll never believe that God does.

What joy I have had during the last ten years, watching so many of the kids I loved and prayed for finally find their way into a growing relationship with Jesus. I am so grateful that the Holy Spirit compelled my devotion to Jesus to not waver in relation to some of the crazy, challenging kids God brought into my life through my own children.

Recently one of these special kids called my son to ask if I would be willing to have lunch with him. Ben knew that I would be happy to. So, as I drove to the lunch, I thought about the decade of prayers for this young man, and now the privilege of being the one he turned to when his soul was in turmoil. As it turned out, that lunch was a critical moment in his journey. Consequently, he was willing to examine his Bozo lifestyle and look at the biblical model of Boaz. This young man ended up in a Bible study and eventually embraced Jesus wholeheartedly. When I watched him get baptized in the ocean, tears poured from my eyes. I was full of gratitude that I didn't give up on him—that I banged on heaven on his behalf for more than a decade.

Let us not become weary in doing good, for at the proper time we will reap a harvest if we do not give up (Galatians 6:9 NIV).

Prayer Requests in a Photo Album

Praying without ceasing for our children and the other children we are blessed to meet is a common activity for a Lady of Devotion, and such an important thing to model for our daughters.

How did I pray consistently for all these kids? It was a holy habit that the Lord led me to develop when my children were very young. For more than fifteen years, I carried kids' names around on index cards I'd inserted into a photo album. Whether I was waiting in line, or picking up everybody at school, or waiting at football practice, or waiting after cheering—the waiting wasn't wasted! I had joy in the waiting as I prayed through the index cards.

Rather than judging so many of these crazy kids, I prayed for them and begged God to start a good work in them and finish it, always praying that they would find God's best—no Bozos or Bimbettes. I would also pray that God would protect my own children who lovingly influenced so many kids from troubled homes. What a blessing it has been to see many of these young people grow up, repent, finally make good choices, and find good spouses.

Prep Quiz Question No. 8: Does your daughter grasp that if she will continue to pursue God's heart, she will attract someone who will encourage her to continue to grow—and they will be each other's spiritual cheerleaders? (See Hebrews 10:24.)

Raising a daughter to be a Young Lady of Devotion who seeks to know God's heart is the very best investment you can make to ensure that she will safely attract a man who also has a connection with God's heart. She will be attracted to those who cheer her on toward God rather than draw her away from Him.

> RAISING A DAUGHTER TO BE A YOUNG LADY OF DEVOTION WHO SEEKS TO KNOW GOD'S HEART IS THE VERY BEST INVESTMENT YOU CAN MAKE TO ENSURE THAT SHE WILL SAFELY ATTRACT A MAN WHO ALSO HAS A CONNECTION WITH GOD'S HEART.

I once heard Miles McPherson (pastor of The Rock Church in San Diego and a former NFL player) say, "When you're looking for a woman, you look for a woman who cheers you on toward God; doesn't pull you away from God."

When he said it, I shouted, "Amen!" It is a classic reality our children need to grasp. In fact, this nugget of truth applies not only to dating but also to friendship. I continually repeat the same questions to the young women I meet across this nation: "Does your boyfriend spur you on to grow closer to God? Or do you find yourself stepping backwards and losing interest in youth group? Are you hanging around your better Christian friends less because of his influence?"

I also ask younger girls, "Does your best friend love Jesus? Is your best friend a growing Christian? Does your best friend know the difference between a Bozo and a Boaz?"

Likewise, Mom, let me ask *you* these questions: Can you name even one girlfriend of your daughter's with whom she would feel at liberty to speak about spiritual things? Does she have a girlfriend whose spiritual growth you can see? Have you overheard conversations between your daughter and her best friend that encourage your daughter's growth spiritually?

Then those who feared the LORD talked with each other, and the LORD listened and heard. A scroll of remembrance was written in his presence concerning those who feared the LORD and honored his name (Malachi 3:16 NIV).

Finally, do you and your own friends engage in the kind of edifying conversation about the Lord that would be recorded in such a heavenly diary?

And let's not kid ourselves. I am sure you know this as well as I do, but sadly, being drawn away from God can happen even in a church youth group. I have discussed with many youth leaders the painful fact that the minute one of your kids stops talking and stops being involved, one of two things is going on: either trouble at home or exclusive dating—dating that has likely entered the physical exploration arena.

You know they're involved physically, because they immediately tend to withdraw from others—hoping for the lights to go down so they can mess around for a few moments. It is amazing how devotional worship time in church (with lights turned down low) can turn into devotion to lustful exploration! All they want to do is explore each other's bodies and see how far they can go. Sometimes all the girl wants is to talk and talk; he just endures it, hoping to get to the making out. But there's no question that the girl is just as likely to be pushing those limits.

We simply have to be alert to these issues in the Church and not hide our heads in the sand. Why do kids like to sit way in the back of church, hoping to be out of clear view of adults? Sure, sometimes it may be to talk and text or play games on their iPhones, but we are naive if we aren't aware of the other games being played!

I was told once about a local youth group that often went to the movies after youth gatherings. When the lights went out, the same gang became so aggressive sexually that the theatre owner called the youth pastor.

Behavior like this requires us to pay close attention to our girls' relationships—even at church. Are the boys drawing our girls away from the Lord or cheering them on toward Him? By the same token, are our girls luring their Christian brothers away from devotion to the Lord or cheering them on? Friends can be the best kind of cheerleaders for each others' spiritual growth; but they can also tease and undermine each others' spiritual lives. Devotion to Jesus has a differentiating impact on whether or not our daughters will be Bozo magnets or Boaz magnets.

Deliver Us From the Kingdom of Self

By definition, to grow in devotion to the Lord is to focus on Him and to seek His heart for His Kingdom. Yet, as we are all too aware, there is another kingdom we like to visit—and camp out in! It is not the beautifully expansive Kingdom of God, but the puny, limited, claustrophobic kingdom of self.

When I became a new Christian, I was introduced to the concept of a life with either *self* in charge or the Holy Spirit in charge. I was constantly asked by my youth leader whether particular behaviors were motivated by self being on the throne of my life, or by the guidance of the Holy Spirit. As the years passed, I heard very little about the impact of self on a person's walk with Jesus, but I was always aware of its obvious manifestation. The Bible clearly defines what this claustrophobic kingdom of self thrives on:

> *The activities of the lower nature are obvious. Here is a list: sexual immorality, impurity of mind, sensuality, worship of false gods, witchcraft, hatred, quarrelling, jealousy, bad temper, rivalry, factions, party-spirit, envy, drunkenness, orgies and things like that...* (Galatians 5:19-21 Phillips).

These activities may look intimidating, yet they are common behaviors of the Me-centric life that is at war with the very life of God within each of His children.

Because we serve the King of kings in a dark and broken world, we are keenly aware of a kingdom that we fight daily. It is a kingdom with walls higher than Jericho and a moat wider than the Pacific Ocean surrounding it. This kingdom is ferociously protected by a warrior that would make Goliath look like a midget.

Many of you might assume that I am writing about the prince of the power of the air (see Eph. 2:2), Satan. Although he is the archenemy of our souls, I am thinking of an insidious enemy that is almost too close to notice:

the enemy called *self.* This is the part of us the Bible calls the flesh, or the "old man." It is the core of self-centered, self-protective sin that compels us, as Paul writes in Romans, to do what the Christlike self does not want to do.

This tyrant of the claustrophobic kingdom of self has harmed our walk with God. However, it is the very work of God in our lives as believers to slay this tyrant and to flourish in our *true* identity, our *true self* in Him. God has given us the spirit of power and love and self-control (see 2 Tim. 1:7); and He has given us the weapons of His Kingdom to aid in our fight.

I have always been aware of the impact of Me-centric living, but recently it has been presented in a powerful refresher course that began when I started reading a book recommended by my son-in-law, Drew. The book, written by Paul Tripp, is entitled, *What Did You Expect?* Here is just a taste:

> In his love, he knows that you are not all that you were created to be. Even though it may be hard to admit, there is still sin inside you, and that sin gets in the way of what you are meant to be and designed to do. And, by the way, that sin is the biggest obstacle of all to a marriage of unity, understanding, and love. God is using the difficulties of the here and now to transform you, *that is, to rescue you from you*[3] (emphasis added).

What a powerful phrase: *"rescue you from you."* Just as I need to be sensitive to my own need to be rescued from the Me-centric lifestyle, as a Mom I need to resist feeding this desire in my child. All one has to do is watch the news about celebrities and notice the enormous kingdom of self that is applauded and aspired to; yet people are shocked when celebrities make poor choices. The kingdom of self is above the law, and the entitlement that fuels this kingdom began in each person's home. Whether among athletes, rock singers, or movie stars, there are many public displays of the kingdom of self for us to see.

From time to time on long trips in the car, I listen to a radio psychologist on Sirius Satellite Radio. A common phrase that always makes me grin is when the radio personality says to a distraught caller, "Now just a minute, I need you to take yourself out of the center of your universe and take a moment to think about this other person."

This counselor continually confronts the claustrophobic kingdom of self dominating the lives of daily callers. So, where do these narcissistic people get their training? Such Me-centric living is in the heart of every man and woman, boy and girl; but it is either enhanced or diminished by those who love them, beginning with those who raise them.

To build up your child's kingdom of self as parents is, ironically, to risk that kingdom exploding into self-sabotaging addictions when the child becomes a teen. The best thing a mom can do in order to limit the feeding of her daughter's demanding spirit is to bravely use that most fearful word: *no*. And by fearful, I don't mean for the child. I have watched an entire generation of parents who seem, themselves, to fear the ramifications of saying *no* to a child.

> THE BEST THING A MOM CAN DO IN ORDER TO LIM-IT THE FEEDING OF HER DAUGHTER'S DEMANDING SPIRIT IS TO BRAVELY USE THAT MOST FEARFUL WORD: *NO.*

Rescue Me, From Me

Being delivered from Me-centric living requires intentionality on the part of the original tutor—good ole Mom. May the thought of your daughter becoming Bozo bait motivate you to say *no* more often than *yes* to your self-centered child. Your daughter will need to practice saying *no* if she is going to be more devoted to Jesus than to the King of Peer Pressure. So Mom, your own use of the word will help your daughter become familiar with it. *No* is a powerful, holy word.

Tragically, I have seen this time and time again throughout decades of life and ministry to women: if you want to make a girl a Bozo magnet, allow her to believe it's all about her. Me-centric girls are so self-focused that they are very resistant to limits. Such resistance to limits shows up in their behavior toward boys.

When a girl is imprisoned in the kingdom of self, she is unwilling to curb her desire for someone who's not good for her. She doesn't want to be told that this good-looking, charismatic guy is a Bozo, because she wants what she wants when she wants it! Sometimes the boy isn't even good-looking or charming, but some other quality attracts her to what is not good for her. Her Me-centric heartbeat cheers her on to get what she wants regardless of the long-term impact. "I want it. I'm entitled to be happy. This guy will make me happy!"

> WHEN A GIRL IS IMPRISONED IN THE KINGDOM OF SELF, SHE IS UNWILLING TO CURB HER DESIRE FOR SOMEONE WHO'S NOT GOOD FOR HER. SHE DOESN'T WANT TO BE TOLD THAT THIS GOOD-LOOKING, CHARISMATIC GUY IS A BOZO, BECAUSE SHE WANTS WHAT SHE WANTS WHEN SHE WANTS IT!

And here is the hard truth for us parents: when we feed this propensity, we become the original drug dealers in our kids' lives. It is astounding to see the kinds of incessant sacrifices parents make to feed the demanding spirits of their children.

So we have to get honest, Mom. We are the ones who let them grow up thinking it's all about them when we *make* it all about them. I hear parents say *all the time:* "I just want my child to be happy." *Happy* becomes the criterion for life rather than the biblical teaching of devotion to Jesus!

Mom: The Original Drug Dealer

I used a term in the previous paragraph that may have thrown you. Yes, it has been said that moms are the original drug dealers—dealing out everything their children want and never saying *no* to their self-consuming appetites.

When a child is young, giving her another toy or cookie satisfies the demanding spirit and escorts her to Happy-Ville; but the older she becomes, the less satisfaction another toy or cookie offers her. The child needs something even more powerful to take her to Happy-Ville. After all the cool clothes and nice cars fail to satisfy, she is vulnerable to drugs.

I have often stated (and this may sound harsh, but please bear with me) that the ultimate abuse is allowing children to grow up thinking the world revolves around them. I am a victim of abuse, so I do not use the term lightly. All seven of my siblings and I were abused by my father. When my dad died I went to his older sister and asked if she had any knowledge of him being abused, *because abusers, if they are not healed, become abusers.* Her response was almost alarming, "Oh yes. Your daddy had the worst abuse. He was the youngest child and was allowed to grow up thinking the whole world revolved around him."

What my aunt was describing to me was the kind of narcissistic mindset that got bred into this man and eventually justified his doing whatever he wanted—even tragically abusing his family. So quite frankly, that's the greatest abuse. That's the core kind of mistreatment of a child that is able to manifest in ways a parent could have never imagined.

I walked away from the conversation with my aunt just weeping. I kept thinking that even I, as a Christian parent, had been so guilty of not wanting to disappoint my child, thus saying *yes* when I should have said *no.*

Our goal as mothers with daughters is to teach them how to continue living when they receive a *no*—to graciously receive it without throwing a temper tantrum or a pity party. And Mom, you can do this! Even if you have struggled with these boundaries or the Lord has shown you things now you had not recognized before, with His guidance, you can help steer your daughter out of the kingdom of self.

One sure path out of that claustrophobic kingdom is to engage your daughter in doing for others. As we discussed regarding diligence in Chapter 2, there are many ways to focus her mind and activities on service rather than on living as a person consumed with what she wants. Praying for her friends is such a selfless act, and this discipline will become foundational in her daily devotion to Jesus. You can encourage your daughter to make up a prayer list of needs in the lives of her friends and to pray through it each night before going to sleep. On this list your daughter can include praying for a growth spurt for the "mean girls" and the "Bozo guys" at her school. This will set her heart toward God's work in others' lives, and He will be faithful in the transformation of *her* mind.

Entitlement Trumps Gratitude

In the book of Ruth, after amazing kindness was shown to Ruth by the stranger, Boaz, her immediate response was "ground-slamming" gratitude. For the entitled, Me-centric girl, amazing kindness and goodness rarely provoke such gratitude for this simple reason: entitlement blinds any capacity to realize that the world does not revolve around her! Teens who skip about in the claustrophobic kingdom of self never notice the loving and kind gestures of those around them, because they see everyone as their willing servants.

How unlike a Young Lady of Devotion such an attitude is! Listen to the words of our model of devotion with her beautiful capacity for gratitude:

> *At this, she bowed down with her face to the ground. She exclaimed, "Why have I found such favor in your eyes that you notice me—a foreigner?"* (Ruth 2:10 NIV)

Ruth's response to Boaz needn't be an exceptional ideal. Gratitude flows from devotion to the one true God. Young people are capable of great unselfishness and devotion to Jesus. We just don't challenge them enough to consider living for something besides humanity's favorite idol—*me!*

> ...somewhere along the way we had missed what is radical about our faith and replaced it with what is comfortable. We were settling for a Christianity that revolves around catering to ourselves when the central message of Christianity is actually about abandoning ourselves.[4]

Recently I had dinner with Chelsea, a young woman whose past was very painful. There were times when I wasn't sure she would recover from the heinous heart wound she had endured. Through challenging her to consider thinking of others rather than "poor me," this precious girl has blossomed into a tender, devoted follower of Jesus.

During our dinner together, I asked her how her fundraising was going for her summer mission trip. She needed to raise $5,000, and said she had all her money and was now helping her best friend to raise her money.

I was so stunned that her funds were already provided. "I was given $5,000 for graduation and I am using it to pay for my trip to Uganda" she replied.

Not only was I blown away that Chelsea used her graduation gift to go on a mission trip (rather than spend it on typical Me-centric toys); but I was also blessed by her passionate commitment to help her friend raise funds for *her* mission trip. Talk about cheering on one's devotion to God!

Chelsea's background could have totally fed the Me-centric idol. She especially could have tried to heal her wounded heart through self-absorption. Instead, this beautiful child is going to a very difficult place this summer to love on children who have had similar heart wounds. Chelsea's spiritual mom has cheered on her devotion to God for a decade, and the results still bring tears to my eyes!

Glory Robber Versus the Lady of Devotion

We had a guest last summer who was such a blessing that her visit seemed much too short. During hours of sharing heart to heart, I told her about a new message I was developing entitled "Glory Robbers." I explained that, although we were created to bring God glory, we constantly rob Him of the glory He is due. Too many Christians have made their lives so Me-centric that they daily rob His glory.

After our wonderful guest left, she pondered the "Glory Robber" theme and she sent the following message:

I was thinking more about being a "glory-robber," and I remembered an illustration that happened to me back in May, and maybe you could use it in your material. Being a glory-robber is like being a bridesmaid who is more worried about making herself look good rather than making sure the bride and groom look good and have all they need. I was a bridesmaid back in May; I just kept thinking that as I watched all of the other bridesmaids getting ready and worrying about how *they* looked and such. I just kept thinking, "No one is even going to be looking at us; we are delusional if at any point in this wedding we think it is about *us* as bridesmaids." And then it ticked me right off when some of this girl's [close childhood friends] who were bridesmaids, were really only conveniently around when the photographers or videographers were around, but they were nowhere to be seen when it was time to take down the reception hall or unload trucks back at home. Glory-robbers often serve the Bride of Christ and the Groom when it is convenient for them or publicity is involved. These were just some thoughts, take it or leave it, just thought I would share.[5]

...everyone who is called by my name, whom I created for my glory... (Isaiah 43:7 NIV).

Let's not be like the delusional, Me-centric bridesmaids in the story above. May we resist the temptation of being "ovation-aholics" and strive to be true servants of the King. Such servants are comfortable with esteeming others as more important than themselves (see Phil. 2:3).

The Young Lady of Devotion knows how to bring glory to God and not rob Him of such glory! May we, by God's grace, raise daughters who are not "ovation-aholics" but God-glorifying Young Ladies of Devotion.

Chapter 5—Questions for Discussion

1. Does your daughter see you modeling hope more often than hopelessness? (See Ruth 1:20-21; Psalms 119:92,147,165.)

2. In relation to the "unfathomable impact of a devoted mom," have you grasped this reality in your own life? Are you distracted by your husband not helping with the spiritual leadership of your family? (See Deuteronomy 6:7-9; First Peter 3:1.)

3. Do you have friends who spur you on in your devotion to Jesus? (See Hebrews 10:24.) Does your daughter, like you, have such a friend, as described in Malachi 3:16?

4. Do you welcome the mission field your children deliver to your door, or do you sometimes resent or fear it? Explain.

5. Discuss creative ways you have reached out to your children's friends with the love of God.

6. Did you or would you make up a photo album of prayer requests on index cards? (See First Thessalonians 5:17; Galatians 6:9.)

7. Do you think you are raising a Me-Centric child? Do you agree or disagree with the idea that moms can become the "original drug dealer"?

8. Do you see your child as more entitled or grateful? (See First Thessalonians 5:18; First Timothy 6:6.)

9. Would you describe yourself as a lady devoted to Jesus or more of a people pleasing "ovation-aholic?" (See Galatians 1:10; Matthew 23:5.) Is your daughter an "ovation-aholic?" Does she lose graciously or is she incapacitated when she doesn't take first place? (See Isaiah 43:7; Philippians 2:3.)

CHAPTER 6

Raising a Young Lady of Purity

Ruth's Purity

When Boaz had eaten and drunk and his heart was merry, he went to lie down at the end of the heap of grain; and she came secretly, and uncovered his feet and lay down (Ruth 3:7).

You may read this at a glance and picture the beginnings of an X-rated scene in Ruth's story. But remember that Ruth was acting according to the customs of the time. She was not slinking into Boaz's bed to seduce him. In obedience to her mother-in-law's instructions, Ruth quietly lay at his feet for him to notice her, thus symbolizing her subjection to Boaz as her nearest of kin.

By doing this Ruth gave him the opportunity, if he so chose, to take legal action for the well-being of her and her mother-in-law. (Without a man, a woman had no form of social security and very few rights in that culture.)

So this was not a brazen act of seduction, but an act of obedience to God's plan for her provision in that day. One thing is certain. When she left to go home, she walked away as a Lady of Purity.

Young Lady of Purity in the 21ˢᵗ Century

Someone might take a look at this section title and exclaim that it's an oxymoron and a completely unrealistic ideal. After all, it's impossible to raise pure girls in such a sex-saturated society. If that were the case, then the biblical illustration of Boaz and Ruth would merely be a fairy tale, an idea that belongs only in a Disney cartoon. However, I wholeheartedly believe that a Young Lady of Purity can live and even thrive in the 21ˢᵗ century. Just as Ruth's purity allowed her to go to Boaz, request that he function as her kinsman redeemer, and exit his presence as pure as she entered, our girls can sustain purity even in a context that greatly challenges their commitment to purity.

Before he left for college, a friend of our daughter's instigated a deeply intense conversation with her. He talked about the respect he had always maintained for her, a respect that he felt her "very being" demanded. He explained that he had not even tried to make a "move" on her because he so respected her purity.

What was so profound about this conversation was that the young man was not a follower of Jesus. When our daughter shared this with me, I was reminded again that a girl's purity is a heart guard, and more than that, it speaks loudly and clearly in the midst of this sex-saturated society.

This heart guard also protected our daughter when she was in college; it does so now, even *after* she is married. A woman's purity is, in fact, a life-long guard of her heart (see 1 Cor. 6:19-20; Prov. 4:23).

> A WOMAN'S PURITY IS, IN FACT, A LIFELONG GUARD OF HER HEART

Sex-Saturated Society

In 1971 I enrolled in a local community college to take some night classes. I had a full-time job, but I wanted to at least begin my college adventure. I signed up for "Freshman Communications," an English class. One of our assignments was to write a paper on something we were passionate about. I was volunteering at the time in a local youth group, and was appalled with the struggles that the young people—Christian kids!—were having in the area of purity.

I was a young Christian myself, and while I totally understood the struggles I had experienced as a non-Christian, Jesus was entirely transforming that former area of bondage. So I was amazed at these kids who had been raised in the Church. I titled my paper *Living in a Sex-Saturated Society.*

When I think about that title today and what is happening in this century, the issues in the 1970s compared to now seem like the Puritan Age versus ancient Greece. I am constantly confronted with levels of sexual perversion that stun me—and I am talking among elementary and junior high school students! We are in a war and we don't even recognize the grenades that are being thrown at our feet!

Prep Quiz Question No. 10: Do you know why teen girls go too far? Would you know how to explain the law of diminishing returns to your daughter and her friends?

MPDP = Mandatory Pre-Dating Prep

Your daughter—every daughter—needs to grasp this mandatory pre-dating prep. It has many aspects, but I would say that most critical to understand is the law of diminishing returns. I know that it may sound like an abstract term, as if I were speaking of physics or some principle in math. However, this principle pertains specifically to our girls' purity. If you are not sure that your daughter has been taught this principle, then this would be a good time in her life to make sure she understands it.

The Law of Diminishing Returns

Do you remember the first time you went somewhere you were just *so* excited about—maybe an amusement park as a kid or a particular restaurant as an adult? All your senses were heightened to take in the experience in as many ways as you could. And it was fabulous! The colors were saturated, the rides were a thrill, the food was incomparably delicious. Now you have gone again...and again. And while you might still enjoy that roller coaster or appreciate the familiar taste of that particular molten chocolate cake, it's not what you would call a thrill anymore.

These are examples of the law of diminishing returns. The return you get from your experience gets less profound or less intense over time.

Certainly you can see how this principle would apply to the challenge of remaining sexually pure. The law of diminishing returns in relation to sex begins with this simple statement: There is no such thing as a non-stimulating caress or kiss. Such affection may seem innocent, but it is rare that it remains innocent. After several sessions of kissing for an extended period of time, the brain-chemical high diminishes, and the couple needs to do something else to attain a comparable high. After all, God made the human body sexually for a particular progression—one that is meant to be followed to its end in the context of marriage. So that very chemistry He wired us with is *designed* to yearn for more.

The Law of Diminishing Returns: Sexual Brinkmanship

Because of how we are created, for all young people, Christian or not, there is a natural progression toward sexual fulfillment. That fulfillment pursued outside of marriage, however, is sin. A couple pushes the limits all the way to the edge—to the brink—and then finds they have gone much too far. This sexual brinkmanship begins with what one assumes is cute and innocent and ends up destroying the relationship. Here is a list that young people move through because of the law of diminishing returns. And let me reiterate, this sexual brinkmanship has no regard for the Christian or non-Christian teen.

Natural Progression Toward Sexual Sin:

1. Look

2. Touch

3. Holding hands lightly

4. Holding hands constantly

5. Light kiss

6. Strong kissing

7. French kissing (entering the No Zone—below the neck—prep for intercourse)

8. Fondling breasts

9. Fondling organs

10. Sexual intercourse

When you consider the law of diminishing returns within the context of a sex-saturated society, a teen can move from #1 to #10 faster than any parent would dream—and in this case, that dream can become a nightmare!

Let me illustrate this law. You drop off your daughter at the mall. Maybe she told you that she was going to meet up with her girlfriends. Maybe she didn't tell you the truth; maybe she lied because the guy she is crushing on invited her to meet him at the mall. As a parent you still feel safe when your child is in public at the mall. But let's be honest: malls and movies are exactly where young people have ample opportunity to move through the list above.

Even if you do know she is meeting a boy there, you think your daughter and this young man are "just going to walk around the mall together." As they are strolling around, he takes her hand. As sweet and innocent as this act of affection may seem, it is very easy for adults to forget the potent physical effect of that first touch. The thrill of this special guy holding her hand can only be compared to a trip to Disney World—fireworks over Cinderella's Castle! I mean, she has an emotional heart attack; she feels electricity flow up her arm the moment he takes her hand in his.

Imagine in our scenario that your daughter has to leave the boy because you are picking her up. So she walks away from him, giddy as a little girl on Christmas morning. She keeps saying to herself, "I can't believe he held my hand." She's so excited she has to call ten friends. Ten times she repeats her delightful experience (if you know teen girls, you *know* I am not exaggerating): "We were looking in the window at Petco. It was *sooo* sweet! There were the cutest little puppies and he just reached over and took my hand!"

Now you may be smiling at this last sentence but the reality of the law of diminishing returns has already set in. (I vividly remember where I was when my husband held my hand for the first time—Six Flags Over Georgia during our last ride together in the park before heading back to our college campus!)

Let's continue the journey to sexual brinkmanship. When your daughter sees this young man again—let's say at youth group—he will take her hand once they are seated together. This time, although she is happy, the fireworks over Cinderella's Castle do not happen. Your girl assumes that the fireworks are stifled by the atmosphere of the youth meeting. Sitting there, she is already planning on duplicating the previous experience by returning to the mall. So the next week, she lies to you again. (Bozo guys often require the girl to lie to arrange to be alone together.)

Saturday arrives and you may be distracted and naïve to the real plan. You drop off your girl at the mall to meet her friends once again. When your daughter spots Mr. Wonderful, he takes her hand and they begin to stroll through the mall.

Yet your daughter is absolutely shocked. When he touches her hand there are no fireworks, no electricity. She wonders, "Is this the same hand?" She has to look at his hand as she ponders the dilemma. Where did the thrill go? Do I not like him anymore? Maybe we need to walk down to the pet store where he first held my hand; maybe seeing those cute puppies will help the thrill return with the memory.

Striving for the Chemistry High

Your teen girl leaves the mall that day completely puzzled by her experience. What she doesn't know is that with physical touch she is always progressing toward a more potent physical thrill. So the next time she and the young man meet at the mall, he puts his arm around her shoulders, pulling her closer to his side, and—guess what?—the fireworks return. The girl is excited and relieved, and feels that their love is here to stay.

> WHAT YOUR DAUGHTER DOESN'T KNOW IS THAT WITH PHYSICAL TOUCH SHE IS ALWAYS PROGRESSING TOWARD A MORE POTENT PHYSICAL THRILL.

Now it's routine. This little couple holds hands, and at the youth meeting he sits with his arm around her. She is elated for this physical display of admiration from her boyfriend in front of all her peers (which many parents may or may not know about at all). Your naïve girl is getting ready for a move toward the No Zone that is inevitable after his next move.

The next step is utterly predictable, as she begins to wonder when he will finally kiss her (thoughts that are almost always egged on by girlfriends, sisters, or even mothers). He "finally" kisses her and the fireworks return; and if that is where it stopped, no parent would have to fear an "innocent little kiss." But the problem is that no kiss is innocent and no kiss is non-stimulating. The next time he kisses her it doesn't have that thrill unless the kissing time is extended. Then kissing isn't as thrilling, so a little tongue is added.

The young couple progresses toward doing more than they ever intended to do. They don't understand that they are actually *marching* toward the No Zone with careless disregard as they engage in activities that deliver them to the sexual brink, and inevitably intercourse.

> THEY DON'T UNDERSTAND THAT THEY ARE ACTUALLY *MARCHING* TOWARD THE NO ZONE WITH CARELESS DISREGARD AS THEY ENGAGE IN ACTIVITIES THAT DELIVER THEM TO THE SEXUAL BRINK, AND INEVITABLY INTERCOURSE.

The fundamental problem is this: most teens have only *heard* that they should not have sex before marriage. Their youth leaders and parents have all said to wait until marriage for sex; but they have rarely had the law of diminishing returns explained to them. They have simply been told "Wait," without explaining how or *why*.

Teens don't understand the mechanics of sex; they don't understand that when you go to the No Zone, you are going too far. That zone was made to be traversed in marriage. Before your kids enter even junior high, you need to share this principle with them. *Read this chapter for family devotions, if you must!* You can begin by saying, "I love you too much not to tell you this. Even if you're going to die of embarrassment, flush red; even if your ears turn blood red, I love you too much not to tell you this."

Even if *you're* going to die of embarrassment, moms! You should've seen me tell my daughter. She almost had a heart attack. But she was like, "Mother, I'm not that type of girl." Of course I'm hoping for that for *all* of our daughters, but we still need to clarify this. In fact, when I was teaching this at Liberty University to all these students, my daughter was in the back listening. She literally said, "I know I used to tease you about it, Mom, but please, you have to warn people. They don't get this."

I know they don't.

Quicker Sexual Brink in the Next Relationship

Something even more terrifying than this slippery slope within a relationship is the reality that when kids date and break up—the next relationship has a built-in accelerator because of previous fooling around. When a girl breaks up with a guy because they fell over the sexual brink, the next time this girl starts dating, the law of diminishing returns almost guarantees her moving faster through the various levels of physical expression. After all, she has already diminished the thrill by going too far in the last relationship, and the chemistry will not be as satisfying on the more "innocent" levels of communicating physically! Consequently a teen can go from simple handholding to aggressive kissing in only one date.

Drawing the Line: Remember the No Zone.

Even the nicest girl you know cannot participate in the behavior on our list and not end up going further than her heart would guide her. God created the No Zone for marriage. Kids think they can play around there and exercise fierce self-control as they reach the end of the list: #10 Sexual Intercourse. Show your daughter the list and let her read where the No Zone is.

Parents can also help their children avoid the No Zone by not permitting their girls to date before they are ready. Recently I found an old transparency I used to display with an overhead projector. It bore the following statistics:

Early Dating and Intercourse

Girls Dating by Age—Intercourse Pre-marriage

- 12-year-olds 91 percent
- 13-year-olds 56 percent
- 14-year-olds 53 percent
- 15-year-olds 40 percent
- 16-year-olds 20 percent

Teens need time to develop their self-control muscles. There have been lots of references over the past few years about the latest research on the development of the brain's frontal cortex. It has been shown that this part of the brain monitors impulse control, but does not fully develop until a person is in his or her mid-twenties. Too many times at mother-daughter events, I meet junior high girls who are already dating and I want to scream, "Do you not have a mother? Is your mother at this event with you?"

Why is it that we have security systems on our homes and totally miss the security system our girls need—boundaries on their emotional craziness! Letting a pubescent, hormonally driven girl go on dates and get into relationships before she is sixteen (and even sixteen is too young for some) is the ultimate insanity.

When our children were teens, they didn't go anywhere unless they were in a group. We would joke and call it "international date night," because the kids were all ages and always traveled in a mob. There was an unwritten rule they all seemed to abide by: no pairing up! What is so great is that by staying in a group and getting to know so many kids, these former teens remain friends today—and they are all in their thirties.

Why Do Christian Kids Go Too Far?

We may not be at all shocked by what goes on in the culture at large. But we have to wake up and be very attentive to the situation in our youth groups and Christian schools. Why are our precious kids acting just like teens in the world? Why are Christian kids getting pregnant? I found an old note that was written at a teen conference in early 2000 that stated:

"Forty-three percent of kids from fundamental churches have had sex by 19 years old." In a 2011 report, according to some research, that percentage has risen to more like 80 percent!

I have three straightforward replies to my questions in the previous paragraph:

1. They get pregnant because they *didn't plan on going all the way!*

2. They are dating too young.

3. They have not developed the muscle of sexual self-control

Scripture is clear "...[a girl] *is a slave to whatever has mastered* [her]" (*2* Pet. 2:19 NIV).

Prep Quiz Question No. 6: Does your daughter know that sex ruins a good relationship or sustains a bad one?

One of the most critical reasons not to have sex before marriage is the emotionally blinding impact of sex on any dating relationship. This blinding reality is a natural consequence that is built in by God. God's will concerning sex before marriage is spelled out in crystal clarity in First Thessalonians 4:3-5:

> *It is God's will that you should be sanctified: that you should avoid sexual immorality; that each of you should learn to control his own body in a way that is holy and honorable, not in passionate lust like the heathen, who do not know God...* (NIV).

This is the will of God: that you abstain from sexual immorality. Bam! Purity is the will of God. No one has to debate it with the youth pastor. It is God's will, no exceptions. And we parents can yell "Amen!" to our heavenly Father's guidelines—*abstain.*

ONE OF THE MOST CRITICAL REASONS NOT TO HAVE SEX BEFORE MARRIAGE IS THE EMOTIONALLY BLINDING IMPACT OF SEX ON ANY DATING RELATIONSHIP.

What our girls need to grasp is that God clearly designed sex for marriage. They need to know that the violation of this boundary on sex blinds them to the context of the Bozo guys they are so "in love with."

This simple concept that *sex ruins a good relationship or sustains a bad one* should be on a Post-it Note on her bathroom mirror before she is prepping for her first date. Right now your daughter may know a girl who is dating a guy who is not good for her. In fact, your daughter has watched this guy be rude to her friend, and she is confused as to why her friend would date such a Bozo. Every time she sees her friend mistreated she finds herself thinking, "Why would she be with him?" She might even be telling herself, "I'd never let a boy talk to me like that." Your daughter is discerning enough to question her friend's choice in a guy, but she needs to know the *why* behind her friend's tolerance of that unloving treatment.

Mom, when your daughter mentions being perplexed about her friend's dating such a Bozo, take her remarks as an invitation to clarify the *why* for her. It is your cue to state, "It is more than likely your friend has become involved physically with her boyfriend."

Your daughter will probably yell, "Mom! How can you say that?"

Then you can run and get this book and share this section with her. You can calmly and lovingly explain that physical involvement makes a girl stay with a Bozo guy, even when her soul is crying, "Get out of this mess!" When a girl allows a guy to move to the No Zone, the bodily involvement becomes like a "hood" over her head, and she can no longer see clearly what a Bozo she is dating. Everyone around her can see it, but she is blinded—and actually trapped—by the hood that she's pulled over her own head!

Sex Ruins a Good Relationship

How does sex ruin a good relationship? When two kids start dating and become involved physically, the innocence disappears and one of their consciences will likely shout—"Get out!"

When I first became a Christian, and had newly exited a sex-saturated dating mentality, I started dating this wonderful Christian guy. His commitment to moral purity touched my heart profoundly. After dating for a year, this young man's moral purity was challenged by a young woman—*me!*

I had assumed the inevitability of moving toward the sexual brink, especially since we were talking about a future life together. I only understood a dating world where sexual sin was actually one of the requirements. When this godly young man broke up with me, I was absolutely devastated. After recovering from the shock, the Lord very kindly brought to my mind a night when this young man and I went too far. We went to the No Zone for a moment—but the moment ended our relationship!

Treat Your Girlfriend As a Younger Sister

I sometimes have an advantage over parents, because young people will ask someone in ministry who speaks frankly questions they would never ask their folks. One question I have heard more times than I can count is this: "How far can we go physically?" Whenever I hear this question, I know they are more concerned about what they can get away with than they are with God's wise design for His Temple—their bodies (see 1 Cor. 6:19-20).

When girls ask me how far is too far, I tell them that First Timothy 5:2 states how far. It says to *"treat younger women with all purity as you would your own sisters"* (NLT).

This passage is speaking to young guys, and it states the boundary on their physical relationships with young women. They are to treat younger women with all purity, as though they were siblings. So you can go as far with her as you do with your sister.

Whenever I say this to teen girls, they yell, *"Gross!"* From heaven's perspective, allowing your boyfriend to go to the No Zone *is* gross. It's all about purity.

> ONE QUESTION I HAVE HEARD MORE TIMES THAN I CAN COUNT IS THIS: "HOW FAR CAN WE GO PHYSICALLY?" WHENEVER I HEAR THIS QUESTION, I KNOW THEY ARE MORE CONCERNED ABOUT WHAT THEY CAN GET AWAY WITH THAN THEY ARE WITH GOD'S WISE DESIGN FOR HIS TEMPLE—THEIR BODIES.

Additional Encouragement to Wait

When our children were six and four, my husband and I were asked to speak at a youth camp in northern Florida. The event took place in the mid-1980s. The leadership wanted us to address the topic of "Why Wait Till Marriage for Sex?" Although we are now three decades beyond this event, the topic has not changed. However, the seriousness of the issue has intensified with our sex-saturated society.

Here is the "Why Wait" list that we shared at that camp. I am sure that you as a parent and mentor are keenly aware of most items on the list. But the painful reality is that most young people grow up hearing that sex before marriage is not God's design, without ever hearing about the high price of premarital sex.

Young people rarely have First Thessalonians 4:3-8 taught to them in youth group. This passage clearly states that God's will for His kids is sexual purity.

So here is the list of consequences of premarital sex—a price tag that is rarely discussed:

1. Suspicion: Am I the only one he has ever done this with?

2. Guilt: A heavy heart of guilt because you are guilty of violating God's design.

3. Fear: What happens if I get pregnant? What if I get an STD? (Note: If guys got the STDs they give to girls, they might develop stronger self-control muscles. Guys spread genital herpes, but they are not impacted by them as profoundly as girls are.)

4. Communication breakdown: Petting begins, and the talking ends. Communication is a key to a good marriage. Exploring each other's body without exploring each other's soul (through communication) is a disaster in the making.

5. Respect/loss of trust: If I can't trust him to exercise self-control before marriage, I can't trust his sexual self-control after marriage.

6. Deception: Being deceived into thinking you're in love, but sex is not love. Eros is blinding.

7. Unfair comparisons: Sex causes you to compare one person with another (damaging memories on file).

8. Post-marital insecurity: Unfaithful husbands were lacking in sexual self-control before marriage. King David never saw the enormous price tag on the back of naked Bathsheba. The presence of physical involvement deceives one into thinking that one is 'in love.'

Never Too Young to Learn About Waiting

Remember the story about sweet six-year-old Nancy Claire and her Bible? (See Chapter 3.) Her mom is making every effort to raise her girl to attract a Boaz and not a Bozo. Someone may think this is nuts—Nancy Claire is only six years old! Well, Bozos don't show up only in the teens. Bozo guys are being groomed by Hollywood's love course, which moms and dads also fall for.

For example, on Valentine's Day, a little boy brought roses and candy to school to give to Nancy Claire. Maybe you are inclined to sigh and think such a gesture is so sweet. But let's give this some critical attention. Who is behind a six-year-old boy giving flowers and candy to a six-year-old girl? *The parents.* So, Nancy Claire's very wise mom decided to handle this based on appropriateness and not sentimentality! She called the mother and told her that Nancy Claire could not accept such an extravagant gift and that she would be bringing it back to the boy the next day at school.

That response may seem cruel to you, but if you were to have a conversation with my sister-in-law you would know this mama was so right. A friend of mine is a vice principal at a Christian school, and the things she tells me about what goes on at the elementary school level are absolutely appalling—things I couldn't print in this book (lest I be sued for slander).

The Bozo guys have arrived in our elementary schools, and their female classmates are already doing things that would have been unheard of in high school when I was a student.

Moms, we need to protect our "Nancy Claires" by not conforming to the sexualized society that is robbing our children of innocence, and infecting them with a vulnerability to sexual sin and compromise.

WE NEED TO PROTECT OUR "NANCY CLAIRES" BY NOT CONFORMING TO THE SEXUALIZED SOCIETY THAT IS ROBBING OUR CHILDREN OF INNOCENCE, AND INFECTING THEM WITH A VULNERABILITY TO SEXUAL SIN AND COMPROMISE.

Here's an example of the kind of activity that happens in schools. While changing for PE class, several fifth-grade girls got the idea to pose in their underwear and have a friend take their picture. This may sound like innocent, playful, silly girl stuff, but the fifth-grader taking the photographs proceeded to show the photo to fifth-grade boys later in the day.

The girls posing in their underwear were all from great Christian homes! There is nothing innocent about the boys who saw their classmates in their underpants and bras. Now the boys have these images in their heads and the girls are either mortified or, as is more and more often the case in our culture, actually excited by the prospect. Culturally we are breeding the God-given sexual shame right out of our girls.

This is not playful puberty games; this is the stuff that stimulates boys in puberty. We then reprimand them for hitting on the girls sexually before they even get to junior high. And this is the stuff that inoculates girls against a healthy and appropriate sense of modesty and embarrassment. Our children are being abused through the daily media flowing into our homes from a sex-saturated society!

Judging Promiscuous Girls Prematurely Robbed of Purity

I have written in other chapters about the need for moms to pray for and witness to the troubled kids God brings into our lives. In our efforts to protect our own girls' purity, it is all too easy to be dismissive of the girls who are already promiscuous.

The development of promiscuity in my own soul was all but inevitable, given that I was assaulted by my neighbor before my dad ever assaulted me, and the abuse went on for years. So I tell moms everywhere that they are called to pray for the girls who are making poor choices sexually. Whenever my children would mention that a girl was promiscuous, I would always ask her name and I would commit to praying for her rather than judging her. I told my kids to pray for her also.

It is so easy to judge rather than pray. I always ask parents to consider the *why* behind her promiscuity. Little girls do not lie in bed and dream about growing up to be prostitutes. Little five-year-old girls do not whisper, "O God, I hope I grow up to be promiscuous!" Are you kidding? Nobody wants to be that. But when children are touched inappropriately and that is stirred up, they believe it is the only thing that gives them value. Be careful about judging such girls; start praying for the healing of the heart wounds that fuel their insecurity and the damaged-goods mentality that produces the ultimate "Bozo bait."

Having written that, it is also worth reiterating that even if we are seeking to teach our daughters to guard against Bozo behavior, it is just as important to pray for the boys who exhibit it. Young men learning to push young women sexually is one part hormones, two parts culture, and three parts sin that has a story behind it.

Bozo guys are as much in need of healing prayers as promiscuous girls are.

21st-Century Sodom and Gomorrah

I am going to make a bold statement that I claim as indisputable. We are living in a 21st-century Sodom and Gomorrah! And I don't need to go far to find evidence of this fact. It comes right into my home on my computer and right into my purse on my cell phone. In a single batch of e-mails, I can receive a darling picture of pajama-clad "princess warrior" Nancy Claire (with her blanket, stuffed, animal, and open Bible) and an e-mail with a subject line that speaks of male genitalia. And yet another e-mail is from a victim of sexual abuse whose predators were church leaders!

So the LORD told Abraham, "I have heard a great outcry from Sodom and Gomorrah, because their sin is so flagrant" (Genesis 18:20 NLT).

I personally cannot imagine the magnitude of the outcry rising up to heaven from this modern Sodom and Gomorrah in which we live.

The extreme contrast between the innocence of Nancy Claire's picture and the "freedom of filth highway" that arrives so freely on my phone makes me physically ill! The smut that is practiced and sent through the airwaves wirelessly is the definition of *flagrant*. How are these terrible things happening so incessantly? Are we Christians so distracted worshiping the "almighty" god of mammon that we casually allow the "freedom of filth highway" to run through the property of our own souls?

> *Therefore come out from them and be separate, says the Lord. Touch no unclean thing, and I will receive you. I will be a Father to you and you will be my sons and daughters, says the LORD Almighty* (2 Corinthians 6:17-18 NIV).

My heart is grieving for the easy contamination of our bodies and spirits (see 2 Cor. 7:1). If there is one, driving reason I write books like this and speak to and with thousands of women each year, it is to encourage, exhort, and *beg* all of us in the Body of Christ to heed this particular call from God to *come out and be separate*. We need to stand out as a people who do things differently than the world—and not least of all in this arena of sexual activity. As Jesus prayed for his followers in John 17:15, it is not that we are taken out of the world, but that we be protected from the evil one and, furthermore, as James writes, we are to remain unstained from the world (see James 1:27). It is through such a witness that people are drawn to hear about the Gospel of liberty for their souls.

> WE NEED TO STAND OUT AS A PEOPLE WHO DO THINGS DIFFERENTLY THAN THE WORLD—AND NOT LEAST OF ALL IN THIS ARENA OF SEXUAL ACTIVITY.

Chapter 6—Questions for Discussion

1. Were you familiar with the law of diminishing returns before reading this book? (See the list on pages 112-113.)

Discuss the progression of sexual sin and the No Zone reality. (See First Corinthians 6:18-20.)

2. Were you surprised by the early dating and intercourse statistics? Discuss the dating age standard in your home. (See First Thessalonians 4:3-8.)

3. Consider the statement that "sex ruins a good relationship or sustains a bad one." Have you had the opportunity to discuss the impact of impurity on a dating relationship? Discuss how sex can "blind" the dating couple, and the built-in consequences it brings! (See Galatians 6:7-8.) Has your daughter mentioned a friend who is dating a Bozo and clearly cannot see him for who he really is?

4. Spend time discussing the many consequences of premarital sex, using the list on pages 121-122. Share with one another which of these high prices you have expressed to your daughter(s). Discuss the following text: *"Flee from sexual immorality. All other sins a man commits are outside his body, but he who sins sexually sins against his own body"* (1 Cor. 6:18 NIV).

5. Has your youth pastor/leader shared the principles from this particular chapter with the youth of your church?

6. Pray for your spouse and for other parents and guardians that you will have the courage to love your daughters enough to share these principles at the appropriate, teachable moments. Prayer will pave the way!

7. Have you been guilty of judging a promiscuous girl, rather than praying for her? Don't forget that Rahab the prostitute was transformed by hope in the God of Israel, and ended up in the lineage of Messiah. You never know when you might be praying for a modern Rahab!

Raising a Young Lady of Security

Ruth's Security

Then he [Boaz] said, "May you be blessed of the LORD, my daughter. You have shown your last kindness to be better than the first by not going after young men, whether poor or rich. And now, my daughter, do not fear. I will do for you whatever you ask, for all my people in the city know that you are a woman of excellence" (Ruth 3:10-11).

Ruth, as a young, widowed woman, must have experienced the lonely longings for the warmth of a husband. But she lived in victory over the desire to "man hunt." Instead of going after the boys, she sat still and let God bring her prince to her. She was a Lady of Security.

In the midst of her circumstances, Ruth could not possibly have seen that a man like Boaz would one day be her prince. Neither can you with your limited perspective see who or where your prince will be. Only God has all things in view.

Surrender to God the terrible burden of always needing life on your terms. God can and will give you His best, if you wait for it.

Ruth not only faced difficult circumstances as a young widow in a foreign land, but she was from a nation that was hardly a favorite of Israel. In fact the men who described her to Boaz would refer to her as "the Moabite"—not at all a complimentary term. Ruth could not change her circumstances nor her nationality as a Moabite; however, she could rest in the true God she had come to trust. Her insecurity was overcome by security in her relationship with God. Ruth hid her insecurities under the wings of the Almighty.

Have mercy on me, O God, have mercy on me, for in you my soul takes refuge. I will take refuge in the shadow of your wings until the disaster has passed (Psalms 57:1 NIV).

Have you as a mom learned to take your insecurities to God and rest in the shadow of His wings? Would those closest to you recognize your security in the One in whom you find refuge? When Boaz had one of his first conversations with Ruth, he referred to her obvious security in resting under the covering of God's wings. This eligible bachelor was fully aware that Ruth had every reason to be insecure, being both a Moabite and a young widow. He made the most wonderful remark about her obvious security:

May the LORD repay you for what you have done. May you be richly rewarded by the LORD, the God of Israel, under whose wings you have come to take refuge (Ruth 2:12 NIV).

RUTH'S INSECURITY WAS OVERCOME BY SECURITY IN HER RELATIONSHIP WITH GOD.

Daughters Reflect Your Security and Insecurities

Growing up, the most obvious model a daughter has is her mother. Moms can model the security they find in the Lord, as Ruth certainly did. We can also model "finding" insecurity in all kinds of things.

My own mom was so focused on certain insecurities that I couldn't help but imitate her debilitating behavior. For example, she was always worried about her weight, and often made comments about other women and their weight. I grew up with this same self-focused insecurity and have battled this unhealthy body image for far too much of my life.

I have a friend whose mother had her and her sister weigh in on the scale every day of their lives. Talk about developing one of the most insecure perspectives of self—especially for us women! Allowing one's weight to determine personal value is just one of the many reasons a girl grows up insecure about how fearfully and wonderfully she is made.

> We spend countless hours in the mirror every week. Fixing our hair or selecting the perfectly flattering outfit. Covering our freckles, highlighting our eyelids, or extending our lashes. We want to be *noticed, admired, loved.* As women created in the image of God, our longing for such approval is natural and I believe actually healthy if it was not for the way human *sinful nature has distorted it.*[1]

Even if your mother did not make you self-conscious about your weight, there is a billion-dollar industry that helps make girls and their moms insecure about their bodies. Although as adults we know that we are being manipulated by the "body beautiful" fashion industry, our self-image still suffers when we compare ourselves to these Photoshopped images that have been digitally manipulated and touched up. Whether it is with movie stars, music icons, or fashion models, the assault is equal opportunity, daily making girls and women doubt that they are fearfully and wonderfully made!

Sadly, even some Christian leaders have succumbed to the "body beautiful" trap and have gone under the knife! In her book *Beauty by God*, Shelly Ballestero notes, "Did you know...that looking at fashion magazines for just 3 minutes lowers the self-esteem of over 80 percent of women, says Dr. Susie Orbach, a leading British psychotherapist?"[2]

Insecurity and a Love Tank Deficit

If a father is absent, your daughter's love tank needs supernatural filling by our heavenly Father. She can become secure in Jesus as He fills her heart deficit. It is not surprising that many of my daughter's friends did not have fathers present in their lives. Whenever I could, I would encourage these fatherless girls to go home and get a Bible concordance and look for all the verses that talk about God as Father. Fatherless girls can have their love tanks filled as they grasp the reality of God as Father.

And do not call anyone on earth "father," for you have one Father, and he is in heaven (Matthew 23:9 NIV).

Papa God can fill the hole left by a father who abandoned his family. Growing in your understanding of the love of God as Father will help fill your daughter's love tank. This is important, because love tank deficits are readily exploited by the enemy. A loser guy can capitalize on a girl's love hunger, because it often produces a craving for male attention and affection. How critical it is for a daughter to become aware that her absent father—whether absent physically or emotionally—can make her more vulnerable to a ravenous hunger for a boyfriend.

A LOSER GUY CAN CAPITALIZE ON A GIRL'S LOVE HUNGER, BECAUSE IT OFTEN PRODUCES A CRAVING FOR MALE ATTENTION AND AFFECTION. HOW IMPORTANT IT IS FOR A DAUGHTER TO BECOME AWARE THAT HER ABSENT FATHER—WHETHER ABSENT PHYSICALLY OR EMOTIONALLY—CAN MAKE HER MORE VULNERABLE TO A RAVENOUS HUNGER FOR A BOYFRIEND.

I am not trying to overwhelm you, but to lovingly address what I have seen for years in the lives of girls whose dads were never there for them. In fact, when I hear parents say, "Oh we've had an amicable divorce," I almost start screaming right on the spot. I wrote the book *Free Yourself to Love: the Liberating Power of Forgiveness*, because by God's grace, I've learned how to forgive the unforgivable. In the book I spell *amicable divorce* a little differently from Webster's Dictionary. I spell it *amica-bull divorce,* because it is absolute bull to say anybody is divorced amicably! It's never good.

Amicable is described as lacking in antagonism. Yet ironically, while the antagonism between the spouses may cease with divorce, the ongoing internal antagonism in each child has just begun. The denial concerning the consequences for our children is inestimable!

Love tank hunger is a very common consequence that enhances a girl's capacity to become Bozo bait. If you are in this situation right now, I want to encourage you: every night before you close your eyes, pray "Oh Jesus, fill my girl's tank." It is a great prayer to cry out in the car as you drive to work or as you put the dishes in the dishwasher. "Fill her love tank, Lord." Mom, God can do it! Let me share some proof of this reality in the heart of a ravenously hungry girl.

When I was just a young teenager, I already had a huge love hunger deficit. Although my parents were not divorced, the abuse I experienced from my father produced a Grand Canyon-sized deficit in the love tank of my heart. As a new Christian reading the Bible for the first time, I came across Matthew 23:9 that states, *"Do not call anyone on earth 'father,' for you have one Father, and he is in heaven"* (NIV).

With childlike faith I claimed God as my only true Father. Forty-six years later, I can still remember declaring, "I claim you Father God as *my* Papa." Still living in an abusive home, I would constantly remind myself of the love of my heavenly Papa.

Praise be to the God and Father of our Lord Jesus Christ, the Father of compassion and the God of all comfort... (2 Corinthians 1:3 NIV).

Father God so filled my love tank that I was able to wait for God's best rather than settle for a Bozo. Secure in God, I waited for my Boaz, whom I've now had for thirty-eight years. So my love tank deficit was compensated by my incomparable Father God.

Oh God, Keep an Eye on Her

One more thing about Papa God I want to share with you. This is a wonderful promise for all moms and their daughters. Whether your daughter has a wonderful relationship with her father or experiences some strain or some neglect, this verse can be a security-building promise of hope. The verse is John 17:11: *"...I am coming to You. Holy Father, protect them by the power of your name..."* (NIV).

In this verse Jesus Christ Himself prayed for your girl. He did it before He left Earth. He asked the Father to guard not only your girl, but also all those who are going to be coming to Christ in the future (see John 17:20).

In John 17:11, the word *protect* means "to guard," or "keep an eye."[3] Jesus, in the garden, asked God Almighty to keep an eye on your girl. So you can pray the same. And when you are asking God to keep an eye on your girl, you are in perfect harmony with God's heart. Matthew 18:19 refers to people agreeing in prayer about specific requests. Agreeing with someone else in prayer is like harmonizing. Well girlfriend, you can confidently harmonize with Jesus concerning His wonderful prayer in John 17:11, saying "Jesus, I agree with You. Keep an eye on my girl." Keep an eye on my girl. Along with your cry for Father God to fill her love tank, you can add *praise* for the fact that God *is* keeping an eye on her.

> God's unfailing love for us is an objective fact affirmed over and over in the Scriptures. It is true whether we believe it or not. Our doubts do not destroy God's love, nor does our faith create it. It originates in the very nature of God, who is love, and it flows to us through our union with His beloved Son.[4]

> YOU CAN CONFIDENTLY HARMONIZE WITH JESUS CONCERNING HIS WONDERFUL PRAYER IN JOHN 17:11, SAYING "JESUS, I AGREE WITH YOU. KEEP AN EYE ON MY GIRL."

Screaming the Truth

"Insecurity among women is epidemic, but it is not incurable. Don't expect it to go away quietly, however. We're going to have to let truth scream louder to our souls than the lies that have infected us."[5]

The father of lies (see John 8:44) screams lies at our hearts daily. We can only scream back if our hearts are wallpapered with the truth (see John 8:32) We, as well as our girls, need to learn how to *scream* at the *liar!* It may seem a contradiction of a *lady* in *waiting* to be screaming, but there are just times when we need to.

When I was a young Christian, I would often have thoughts of worthlessness. I can remember when I first began to exercise appropriate screaming at the enemy of my soul. I was walking to my car after sharing my heart with some teen girls, and as I was backing my car out of the church parking lot I had this thought: "If those girls knew what a loser you really are, they would never listen to you!"

I can still feel how quickly those tears came to my eyes and how swiftly the thoughts of worthlessness poured into my heart. But as quickly as this attack of insecurity invaded my soul, I remembered a verse that I had just learned, Revelation 12:10-11:

> *...For the accuser of our brothers, who accuses them before our God day and night, has been hurled down. They overcame him by the blood of the Lamb and by the word of their testimony; they did not love their lives so much as to shrink from death* (NIV).

As I thought about the 24/7 lying accuser of all Christians, I—as boldly as a teenager could—screamed, "You can go back to where you belong because I belong to Jesus and His blood is my confidence!"

That screaming moment in my car became a confidence framework for the many times in the future when I would face demonized accusations, and would overcome the liar with the scream of truth! Let me share a glimpse of the confidence that allows me to scream back at the assaults of insecurity that plague all women—young and not so young.

With God, Who Could Be Against Her?

Have you ever been criticized so harshly that the pain knocked the breath right out of you? I lived in a household where this was part of the daily schedule! One day a godly woman said to me, "Whenever you are criticized, consider the source, and that will help you monitor your reaction."

I thought a long time about the expression, "consider the source," and I became so excited about this *fact*: God, who knows me through and through, still chose me for Himself.

God's foreknowledge did not keep Him from choosing a sinner like me. Without foreknowledge, people make some serious mistakes, but God, who is all knowing, never makes mistakes and is never caught off guard. This all-knowing God did not choose against me, but for me.

Whenever I am criticized, I first ask the Lord to show me any aspect of the criticism that may be truth, so I can repent and let Jesus transform that blind spot in my life. When the criticism contradicts something that Jesus says about me, I choose to value Jesus' opinion rather than people's opinions. Whatever people say about me, I accept; but I lay the comments alongside Jesus' biographical sketch of me, because that is where I live, rest, and have confidence. Jesus' biographical sketch for one of His girls would read something like this:

- She is chosen and dearly loved by *Me* (see 1 Thess. 1:4; Col. 3:12).

- She is a child of *Mine*, part of *My* family (see Rom. 8:15-16).

- She is free to call *Me* "Daddy" (see Gal. 4:6).

- She was on *My* mind before I spoke the world into existence (see 2 Tim. 1:9).

- She is a one of a kind, custom designed by *Me* (see Eph. 2:10).

- She is getting better with every passing moment (see 2 Cor. 5:17).

- She is part of a royal calling and responsibility (see 1 Pet. 2:9-10).

- She is an heir of an unshakable Kingdom (see Gal. 4:6-7; Heb. 12:28).

- She is aware of her enemy, but is dauntless (see 1 Pet. 5:8).

The next time someone speaks to you in a harsh and critical manner, just pause and think: *Excuse me; do you know with whom you are speaking?* That thought always puts a smile on my face (which puzzles the one who would slay me verbally).

> WHATEVER PEOPLE SAY ABOUT ME, I ACCEPT; BUT I LAY THE COMMENTS ALONGSIDE JESUS' BIOGRAPHICAL SKETCH OF ME, BECAUSE THAT IS WHERE I LIVE, REST, AND HAVE CONFIDENCE.

Why do we continue to allow people's rejection (or imagined rejection) to control us more than the acceptance we have received from God Almighty through Jesus?

In face of all this, what is there left to say? If God is for us, who can be against us?... (Romans 8:31 Phillips).

A number of years ago, I heard the psychologist Dr. Leslie Parrot use a term that perfectly describes how an insecure person is motivated. She coined the term "a compulsion for completion," defined as such:

If you try to build intimacy with another person before you have done the hard work of becoming whole on your own in Jesus, then all your relationships become an attempt to complete yourself, and it sets you up for failure.

A girl who is confident in the love of God and the love of her family will not struggle with a debilitating compulsion for completion. In the next section, I will expand the discussion from Chapter 6 about a particularly damaging place young women go when they are compelled by such compulsions.

Prep Quiz Question No. 9: Does your girl (tween/teen) know about the No Zone and about staying out of it? Did you know that insecurity escorts many girls to the No Zone?

Too often we assume that teen girls make poor choices in relation to sexual sin merely because they are lacking in morals. I would argue that such quick jumps to judgment are not fully accurate. Such great numbers of teen girls become involved sexually because they are insecure. Some are not secure enough to resist the advances of their boyfriends, and others mask genuine insecurity by becoming sexually aggressive toward boys. None of these girls are secure enough to swim upstream against society's flagrant immorality.

Let me share a story. I know of two ninth-grade girls who attended two separate slumber parties. At one party, the older girls told the younger girls what they needed to do in order to date the popular guys on campus. The common requirement was a visit to the No Zone sexually. That would get a girl a date with the BMOC (Big Man on Campus).

A very insecure girl heard these remarks, took a deep breath, and bravely took trips to the No Zone in order to date the cutest guy on campus. She would cry after trips to the No Zone because her conscience would remind her that such trips did not please God. But she was not secure enough to say no. She was not secure enough to be "dateless" and outside the "cool crowd."

Another ninth-grader went to a slumber party where she heard a contrasting message to the previous one. This ninth-grader heard about being a Ruth and waiting in purity for God's best. This girl was secure enough in God's love and her family's love to make a vow in her heart to remain pure and wait. Her security allowed her to remain so until she married—which wasn't until she was forty. Yes, she was a forty-year-old virgin!

I wish I could say that I was the secure girl, but I was the girl in the first story. My deep insecurity and impatience plunged me regularly into the arms of Bozo guys who enthusiastically escorted me to the No Zone.

Timeline for Dating

Too many girls start dating *way too early.* How do I know that? I have met thousands of girls who regret going too far sexually when they were teenagers. These girls were not secure enough to date. Their parents bent to peer pressure and chronology as the qualifying criteria for dating.

The dating timeline is not a rigid formula. If your child cannot say no without worrying about what her friends think—over a movie or music or certain activities—then she is *not ready to date.* The ability to say no is inextricably linked, not only to the virtue of your child, but the security of your child.

You know what my daughter (now a pastor's wife) says? "It's so simple, mother, tell girls to keep their clothes on."

This is the kind of thing we *must* tell our daughters and their girlfriends. "You know how not to fool around before marriage? You don't take your clothes off."

It's really hard to have intercourse with all your clothes on. It's really hard for a guy to fondle you with your clothes on. It's not a turn-on for him because he doesn't touch anything real. Fully clad girls will not be visiting the No Zone. Bozo guys date because they want to go to the No Zone. At the ninth-grade slumber party I attended, the older girls showed the younger girls *how to help the guys undo their bras!*

This particular slumber party was in 1965: A room full of insecure girls instructing even more insecure younger girls on how to become Bozo bait and spend time fishing in the No Zone!

The Gift of "No"

The capacity to say no is really the key to when one's daughter is ready to date. In fact her ability to say no to a young man's advances physically is actually a "gift": she not only gives it to herself, but also to the young man. In the book *To Own a Dragon*, Don Miller validates this remark:

> Women saying no to men, not letting men have sex with them, causes men to step up....I think men need women to be women, and we need to be made to jump through some hoops. If a woman withholds sex until she gets what *she* wants, we are all better for it....A girl is actually blessing her guy when she says no. She is enhancing his inner world and strengthening his potential to leave his adolescence."[6]

Now consider the following question:

Prep Quiz Question No. 1: Do you know why older guys date younger girls?

The painful answer to this question is this: insecurity attracts predator guys. Older guys know that younger girls are easier to seduce. Younger girls are so in awe of older guys because their insecurity over-inflates their image of them. That is bad enough, but I literally have been in the presence of a mom who is excited because a senior on the football squad paid attention to her freshman daughter.

When I hear things like this, I am ready to find a large cooler of Gatorade, pour it on the mom, and hope she will come to her senses!

Younger girls at mother-daughter events often tell me about dating older guys. I always ask, "Is your mom at this event?"

Then the young girl will say, "Why do you want to know?"

I boldly tell the child, "I am going to go and find your mom and smack her right upside her head!" The teen always laughs, but my heart is not laughing. I am devastated for the vulnerable situation this mom has carelessly exposed her daughter to!

Just recently I had an adorable little freshman e-mail me and say, "Oh Mrs. Kendall. I'm having a new experience. I never dated in high school, but I've only been on this campus three weeks and a senior is texting me all the time. He's so nice, and I'm so stunned that a senior is giving me such attention."

I screamed at my computer, "Girlfriend! This senior has used up all the other girls before you came to college and he is looking for a new batch to use during his final year on campus."

This is no different from the high school stories I hear. It's just in a different location without parents knowing about it.

I'm blown away when parents talk about four-year-olds having crushes on each other. When I hear foolish remarks like this, I want to throw myself on the floor and act like a four-year-old! I want to throw a temper tantrum and scream at these parents that they have a responsibility to not hurry their children into crushes and going steady! Not surprisingly, parents who don't intentionally monitor this acceleration end up being some of the same parents who are shocked when their fourteen-year-old is pregnant.

Here is what is going on: Our society is accelerating the sexuality of our children. But moms, we need to battle to keep it reigned in as long as possible! Social media sexualize our children prematurely; we cannot complacently stand by as though we have no influence. And I'm telling you, long before there were computers in every house and phones in every palm, I had to fight against this, too. My husband and I were like salmon swimming upstream. We were in a good church and great Christian school, but we knew a lot of parents who were mentored by Hollywood rather than the Bible.

So Ken and I had dating and relating standards that were not always like those of other parents. Our kids would come home and say, "Well Andrew's parents are letting him go."

I would reply, "I'm sorry to hear that. Daddy and I love you too much to say yes."

I would often say to our children that it was our love for them that gave us the courage to say no to their enthusiastic pleading!

> ## OUR SOCIETY IS ACCELERATING THE SEXUALITY OF OUR CHILDREN.

Source of Insecurity for *All* Teen Girls

If a teenage girl has a pulse, she will have daily skirmishes that threaten her security. No matter how much a girl is loved by parents and siblings, there are inevitable things that will cause her to worry. Here is a list that was the result of interviews with teen girls age twelve to fifteen. The girls were asked to share the things they worried about. This list is a reminder for all moms to pray for the development of a Young Lady of Security.

- Girls talking about me
- What other people think about whatever you're doing
- If my friends are really going to be my friends around other people
- If I get in a fight with my friends, are we going to hate each other and become rivals?
- Spiders
- Grades
- Boys
- Friend situation (who is being mean)
- Rumors
- Succeeding in school and in general
- Trying to be good at everything
- Trying to make myself worth someone's time
- Fighting with siblings
- Loneliness

- Screwing up my life and not realizing it

- That people will think I'm weird

- Not making the right choices

- Gaining weight

- If people judge me from my appearance

- That I won't know how to get out of a bad situation

- Getting into trouble[7]

These results are reflective of a teen girl's fear of what others think of her and how she views herself. I wonder how many of the statements in this list are also a struggle for her mom. Remember that our girls mirror our insecurities. Throughout my daughter's teen years, I would often cringe when I would see a glaring insecurity in my daughter that was a "clone" of my own people-pleasing struggle!

Secure Enough to Face Bullies and Mean Girls

I have to say that I am actually grateful for the "tutorial" in relation to mean girls that I received during our daughter's teen years. It was often painful but so informative. Together she and I learned so much in relation to jealousy, or being at war with the good in another (see Acts 13:45).

We also learned a lot about forgiving the emotional terrorists (bullies and mean girls) she sometimes faced. If I, as a Christian mom, wasn't committed to forgiving others, I might have ended up in the news—a screaming mom shown strangling teen girls who were so hurtful without a cause! Some mean girls in our daughter's school wrote the "b word" under her picture when it was displayed somewhere at school.

One school year during spiritual emphasis week, a group of girls came and asked Jessi to forgive them for the mocking they had done for years behind her back. You may wonder what they were mocking her for. These girls admitted mocking Jessi for winning back-to-back awards for Best School Spirit and Class Spiritual Leader!

So Jessi was mocked because of her joyful love for her school and her Lord. Being at war with the good in another person is unfortunately human nature, and we all need to examine our own struggles with envy and jealousy toward the good in others.

How early does bullying begin? Do mean girls only develop with the hormonal flood of puberty? I got this e-mail from a mother concerned about bullying in kindergarten!

> I hope you're including an entire chapter on bullying/mean girls—and it has already started in Kindergarten! When Yancey Jr. was in kindergarten, there were a couple of instances with some first grade boys and I really thought it was isolated until Nancy Claire came home telling about bullying by girls during the last two weeks. Not knowing if she was being dramatic or telling the truth, I e-mailed her teacher. They've had talks with two girls who are bullying others in the class! My heart was broken listening to her talk about it but I also held out hope that she was just vying for a little extra attention. I am sad to know that's not the case.[8]

I have included my reply to this bullying/mean girl situation simply because it is my heart's passion to encourage moms to be wise cheerleaders for their children, so they can make good choices in a world where bad choices are too common.

Here is my letter to Kristi:

Dear Kristi:

Bullies are EMOTIONAL TERRORISTS...Mama...grab your precious Nancy Claire's hand each night and start praying for these bullies! Prayer can do what God can do. And it will help your daughter see God as her defender—with the co-defender of an attentive mother!

These girls are not secure enough to love others...their insecurity results in their being at war with the good in our children!

We need to make sure our girls are secure in the love of God and their family, which will help fortify them when the bully says things that are mean...

Two family therapists I greatly respect remarked on bullying with true wisdom.

Unfortunately, despite prevention and education, girls will most likely still be mean. Your daughter will still be hurt. This is where we return to your role. Give her a safe place to come home where she feels unconditionally liked and loved. When she can't say it with words, watch for signs that she is hurting: stomachaches before school, shyness around certain kids, headaches after church.... Let her try to handle it on her own first—but if the situation continues to escalate, step in. Then call the teacher, the school counselor, or whatever adult is in a position to help.[9]

During mean-girl and mocking Bozo-boy encounters, I knew that our daughter needed to develop a most significant capacity. This capacity can bring good out of evil and transform such difficult trials into a mission field! The following section describes what we learned about God's redemptive work in the midst of hurtful bullying experiences.

> PRAYER CAN DO WHAT GOD CAN DO. AND IT WILL HELP YOUR DAUGHTER SEE GOD AS HER DEFENDER—WITH THE CO-DEFENDER OF AN ATTENTIVE MOTHER!

Forgiving Bozo Guys and Mean Girls

Children who are coached in how to ask forgiveness and how to give forgiveness will be a pleasure to be around their *entire* lives.

Here are a few coaching tips for teaching your child how to be a good forgiver:

1. Let your daughter articulate the grievance, offense or hurt (*i.e.,* being embarrassed by someone in class).

2. Ask your daughter how it made her feel. (You are using this situation for healing and instruction in loving freely—which is forgiving freely.)

3. Ask your daughter to name a "hero." Then encourage her to do something truly "heroic"—to forgive this person for hurting her feelings.

4. Encourage your daughter to pray with you, because to pray for the offending person is to overcome evil with good (see Rom. 12:21). Pray that God will bless this person and make him or her more like Jesus. (Note: You can't fail when you pray with your child. In fact, the only failure in prayer is to not pray.)

5. Remind your daughter after praying for the offender that this prayer was a truly heroic act—to pray blessings on those who hurt you is using the "super power" of Jesus in you!

These tips on forgiving also apply to mean teens. Some teenagers are so mean they emotionally "eat your child for breakfast" when arriving at school. Parents can miss the chance to tutor their teens in how to forgive these mean kids by praying for them. Praying for those who hurt innocent kids is a noble and heroic mission; in fact, those mean kids are a critical mission field in our kids' lives.

Remember, as parents, we need to practice these things as much as our children. Being offended is inevitable, but staying offended is a choice. A healthy family is a place where failure is not fatal and where forgiveness is given as freely as hugs and kisses (see Rom. 12:19-21; Eph. 4:32).

Being loved and encouraged by her family cultivates a security that is second only to your daughter's security in her salvation in Christ. These are the foundations upon which to build as you raise a Young Lady of Security.

Chapter 7—Questions for Discussion

1. Does your daughter mirror any of your insecurities? (See First Corinthians 11:1; Psalms 139:14.)

2. Is your daughter struggling with a love tank deficit due to an absent father? (See Matthew 23:9.)

3. Discuss Jesus asking God to "keep an eye on" you and your daughter (see John 17:11,20).

4. Does your daughter know enough Scripture to "scream" the Word at the lies that challenge her security? (See John 8:32,44; Psalms 139:14; Ephesians 1:4-5.)

5. Read and discuss the quote by Donald Miller in the section titled, "The Gift of 'No'" (see 1 Thess. 4:3-8).

6. Did you know why older guys date younger girls? (See First Timothy 5:1-2.)

7. Discuss how insecurity escorts teens to the No Zone (see 1 Cor. 6:19-20).

8. Is your daughter secure enough to say "No" when pressed to enter the No Zone?

9. Does forgiving the Bozo guy or mean girl seem a ridiculous request? (See Romans 12:19-21; Ephesians 4:32.)

Special Mother-Daughter Bonus Activity

Replace Insecurity With a New Sense of Competence

Here is an activity that you and your daughter can do together. Put the following confidence-building truths on index cards to have on the nightstand by your bed. You both would be blessed by having these truths close by. They will be readily available to glance at before going to sleep at night.

After a long day of dealing with emotional terrorists, these cards will be a refreshing reminder of the truth about not only your daughter but you as well!

Eleven Truths to Strengthen Security and Defuse Insecurity

We...are being transformed into the same image from glory to glory, just as from the Lord, the Spirit (2 Corinthians 3:18).

TRUTH #1— DO NOT LABEL YOURSELF NEGATIVELY.

- Self-condemnation leaves no room for loving others.
- If you're hard on yourself, you're hard on others.

...Love your neighbor as yourself (Matthew 22:39).

TRUTH #2—BEHAVE ASSERTIVELY, WITH GOD CONFIDENCE.

- God confidence is the opposite of arrogance and pride.

For God did not give us a spirit of timidity, but a spirit of power, of love and of self-discipline (2 Timothy 1:7 NIV).

TRUTH #3—WHEN YOU FAIL, CONFESS, AND REFUSE TO CONDEMN YOURSELF.

- If you fail, it only means you still have a pulse.

*If we confess our sins, he is faithful and just and **will forgive** us our sins...* (1 John 1:9 NIV).

There is now no condemnation for those who are in Christ Jesus... (Romans 8:1 NIV).

TRUTH #4—DO NOT COMPARE YOURSELF WITH OTHERS.

- Comparisons are demoralizing.

- You are a unique, one of a kind; therefore you are incomparable.

...When they measure themselves by themselves and compare themselves with themselves, they are not wise (2 Corinthians 10:12 NIV).

TRUTH #5—CONCENTRATE ON GOD'S GRACE.

- A definition of grace: for one to bow down in order to benefit another/others greatly.

- Grace is strength allotted to me to behave myself.

How great is the love the Father has lavished on us, that we should be called children of God! And that is what we are!... (1 John 3:1 NIV).

TRUTH #6—ASSOCIATE WITH POSITIVE PEOPLE.

- As we associate, we become.

- Your closest friend is a mirror of the future you!

He who walks with the wise grows wise... (Proverbs 13:20 NIV).

Truth #7—Learn How to Rejoice in All Things.

- The key facet of emotional health is the ability to be thankful and grateful.

Give thanks in all circumstances, for this is God's will for you in Christ Jesus (1 Thessalonians 5:18 NIV).

Truth #8—Have Realistic Expectations of Yourself and Others.

- Remember, on your best day...you are still "but dust" (see Ps. 103:13-14).

- The source of so much grief: unrealistic expectations (see Ps. 39:7).

...Do not think of yourself more highly than you ought, but rather think of yourself with sober judgment... (Romans 12:3 NIV).

Truth #9—Growth and Change Are a Process, and Are Never Instantaneous.

- God is the Agent of Change (see John 17:17).

- The start is the promise of the finish (see Phil. 1:6; 1 Thess. 5:24).

- In God's corrections, He never stops believing in us!

For whom the Lord loves He reproves, even as a father, the son in whom he delights (Proverbs 3:12).

Truth #10—Do What Is Right & Pleasing to Jesus.

- Pleasing Jesus is not the same as pleasing people (see Matt. 6:1).

- How do you discern the difference between people pleasing and "Papa pleasing?" (See Hebrews 4:12-13.)

...If I were still trying to please men, I would not be a servant of Christ (Galatians 1:10 NIV).

Truth #11—Be Positive.

- Consider fasting from critical remarks.

- See how long you can go without saying something negative.

- Pray for a mouth filter:

*Finally, brothers, whatever is true, whatever is noble, whatever is right, whatever is pure, whatever is lovely, whatever is admirable—if anything is excellent or praiseworthy—**think about such things** (Phi-lippians 4:8 NIV).*

Raising a Young Lady of Contentment

Ruth's Contentment

If you consider the circumstances, Ruth had the perfect excuse to be discontented. Her circumstances, including widowhood at a young age, provided the perfect breeding ground for self-pity and bitterness.

Yet Ruth chose to cling to the God of Israel, whom she found to be trustworthy even in difficult circumstances. Contentedly facing each day's task, Ruth received the attention of the most eligible bachelor in town.

Then Naomi said, "Wait, my daughter, until you find out what happens. For the man will not rest until the matter is settled today" (Ruth 3:18 NIV).

"Wait." Such an assignment is not given to cause suffering, but to prevent it. Women experience so much needless pain when they run ahead of God's format. Naomi did not want Ruth's heart to race ahead into disappointment in case the circumstances did not go as they expected.

Discontentment Suffocates Joy

When we find ourselves discontented, we are all too often focusing on what is missing from our lives rather than seeing what is going well with them. Ruth could have focused entirely on being a young widow. She could have walked about Bethlehem in a constant, self-focused mourning state. But this is not the picture we are given in Scripture. Ruth trusted God with her circumstances and went about working in the barley harvest rather than focusing on "poor me."

Too many girls think they are joyless because they are "boyfriend-less." The irony is that they are joyless because they are not content with God's will for their lives.

Comparing one's life circumstances with others' is always suffocating. Discontentment is fed by unfair comparisons. When a teenager compares anything about herself with another girl—even if the girl is her best friend—comparison will always suffocate her joy. Paul the apostle warned us about this discontentment that flows from foolish comparisons.

For who makes you different from anyone else? What do you have that you did not receive? And if you did receive it, why do you boast as though you did not? (1 Corinthians 4:7 NIV)

The archenemy of contentment is self-pity. For many years I viewed self-pity as emotional weakness. Then a godly man corrected my perception. I learned that self-pity is just inverted pride, and pride is never weakness. When people feel discontent and sorry for themselves, they are angry because they didn't get what they wanted. Pride feeds an overinflated view of what one deserves.

Self-pity is easily the most destructive of non-pharmaceutical narcotics; it is addictive, gives momentary pleasure and separates the victim from reality.[1]

Ask Jesus to help you not allow the emotional vampires of discontentment and self-pity to drain you of your joy in the Lord.

> WHEN PEOPLE FEEL DISCONTENT AND SORRY FOR
> THEMSELVES, THEY ARE ANGRY BECAUSE THEY
> DIDN'T GET WHAT THEY WANTED. PRIDE FEEDS AN
> OVERINFLATED VIEW OF WHAT ONE DESERVES.

Contentment and Holy Sweat

If Ruth had been consumed with discontented self-pity, she would never have volunteered to work in the hot sun in a barley field. Discontentment would have kept her at home pouting about her circumstances, and she would have missed not only God's provision of food for her and Naomi, but also the divine appointment of meeting her Mr. Right.

> *And Ruth the Moabitess said to Naomi, "Please let me go to the field and glean among the ears of grain after one in whose sight I may find favor." And she said to her, "Go, my daughter"* (Ruth 2:2).

Notice that Ruth said, *"Let* me go to the field and glean." Ruth was asking for the privilege of meeting not only her own need but also Naomi's needs. Ruth's contentment allowed her to do something hard for a greater good. She had no idea the profound impact of her contented choice. Serving others is a perfect escort out of self-pity and will enhance one's contentment.

> Doing nothing for others is the undoing of one's self. We must be purposely kind and generous, or we miss the best part of existence. The heart that goes out of itself gets large and full of joy. This is the secret of the inner life. We do ourselves the most good doing something for others....[2]

Encouraging your daughter to do for others as a Young Lady of Diligence, further develops her into a Young Lady of Contentment, qualities that will deeply bless her and strengthen her joy (see 1 Tim. 6:6).

Contentment and Boredom

Contentment is a learned character quality. The teen years provide many opportunities to "learn contentment." As a mom, you can be a great coach in developing a more content daughter. Consider this alternative to a teen's boredom: The next time your tween/teen mentions that she is bored, don't concern yourself with how to end her boredom. Instead ask her to think of something she can do for someone else. When she thinks of something to do for another, encourage her to do that very thing! Your cheerleading will help her step out of boredom and into joy.

My youngest brother called me one day and was so excited that I could hardly make out what he was shouting. I asked him to repeat what he said. His reply was, "Jackie, I now know without a doubt why you are such a happy person. I just heard President Clinton say, 'People who live to serve others are the most satisfied of people.' You have spent the last four decades serving others, and you are the most satisfied person I know!"

...he [or she] *who refreshes others will himself be refreshed* (Proverbs 11:25 NIV).

Prep Quiz Question No. 13: Is your teenager mildly content or an incessant whiner? Me-centric girls are "Bozo bait"… one selfish teen attracting another and wanting instant gratification.

Teenagers do not have a monopoly on whining. It's an ancient human behavior. Simply read chapters 11 and 14 of the Book of Numbers and you will not only encounter thousands of people whining, you will see the serious consequences of it. For a parent, whining is like fingernails dragged down a chalkboard. It can be emotionally excruciating to a tired parent (and let's face it, at one time or another, all parents are tired).

Years ago I heard a friend say, "Whining is just anger squeezed through a tiny hole." As I thought about her definition I decided it was one of the best I have ever heard. Teens as well as adults whine and complain when they are disappointed. You may wonder what disappointment has to do with anger. Well, shortly after someone is disappointed, a secondary emotion arrives on the scene; that emotion is anger. So when a teen doesn't get what she wants or senses she is not going to get what she wants, she is disappointed and then she is angry and then her lips are pursed for the burst of whining—anger squeezed through a tiny hole!

> YEARS AGO I HEARD A FRIEND SAY, "WHINING IS JUST ANGER SQUEEZED THROUGH A TINY HOLE." AS I THOUGHT ABOUT HER DEFINITION I DECIDED IT WAS ONE OF THE BEST I HAVE EVER HEARD.

If you look at the Prep Quiz Question above, you'll see the reference to the whining girl being easy Bozo bait. That is because whining is the sound of a person wanting life on his or her own terms. The Bozo guy wants life on his terms, and he is attracted to a girl who has the same life goal—it is all about me! Whining is like the native tongue of the Me-centric teen, and Me-centered girls are alluring Bozo bait. One selfish teen attracts another, and their commitment to themselves ultimately ends in disaster. When they break up, it's a whining mess; it's like an accident scene of blame, each complaining that the other didn't give what he or she wanted!

This kind of accident requires a special rescue vehicle, what friends of mine used to call a *whambulance*—the ambulance for whiners! In their tiny universe of self-absorption they will ultimately need to be rescued from their wreckage. Such complaining and whining flows from not getting life on one's own terms; and the only antidote to this debilitating condition is learning the secret of contentment, as expressed by the apostle Paul:

> *Not that I speak from want; for I have learned to be content in whatever circumstances I am. I know how to get along with humble means, and I also know how to live in prosperity; in any and every circumstance I have learned the secret of being filled and going hungry, both of having abundance and suffering need. I can do all things through Him who strengthens me* (Philippians 4:11-13).

Limit Self-Indulgent Emotionalism (Whining Versus Whatever)

The unappreciative heart is always miserable. Does your daughter whine almost incessantly? I know parents who have girls who don't smoke or drink or run with the wrong crowd, but are constant whiners. Here is a very sober warning to Christian parents: This may look innocent in comparison to teen drinking, but let me tell you, the Word of God is very clear about the heart issues that whining indicates. You need to pray about your daughter's whining problem.

Jesus Himself stressed the importance of the issue in Luke 6:45:

A good man out of the good treasure of his heart brings forth good; and an evil man out of the evil treasure of his heart brings forth evil. For out of the abundance of the heart his mouth speaks (NKJV).

Just consider the fact that God judged Israel in the wilderness because of their faithless whining.

The words we speak reveal the state of our hearts. In turn, the quality of our lives reflects the gratitude of our hearts. I am completely convinced that if God killed people today for whining, churches would be fairly empty. I'm very serious about that. We are all Egyptian-delivered whiners.

Would your home be described as a No Whining Zone? Or is whining the 24/7 background music at your house? Mothers and daughters can create a No Whining Zone together by learning the serious impact of whining on one's life. In our home, I would constantly say, "I can't hear you when you are whining!"

Ironically, too many people employ whining as an emotionally persuasive language. Too many parents either ignore whining altogether or comply with its demands. Whining doesn't end with the expiration of childhood; we all know plenty of adults who are habitual whiners. Are you thinking of a particular one right at this moment? When an adult whines, it is like an emotional temper tantrum.

One of the worst aspects of whining is that it is a contagious habit. When you take the time to read about the whining in the wilderness, the complaining began with ten men and moved to thousands (see Num. 13:32; 14:1-2; Josh. 14:8). Does your daughter have a friend who enhances her whining or challenges her whining? I know that parents are concerned that their children do not engage in crude speech, but I have yet to meet a parent who is concerned about their discontented, whining teen! Maybe our homes should have a *no whining jar.* Then offenders would be required to deposit a quarter every time they whine. The proceeds can go to missions!

Self-indulgent emotionalism allows whining to exist without making an effort to learn a better habit of contentment. Whining is a habit, and learning to be content is a great habit to replace it. My daughter's whining used to drive me crazy, until I realized that this "native tongue of whining" was learned from the other woman in the house—*me!*

As I began to study the seriousness of whining and the source of whining, I began to seek the Lord for a word to remind me to resist indulging in this. I had read many articles on worship being an antidote to depression. (I liked the word *worship* because it started with a "w" like whining did.) Then one day when I was reading about a teenager who replied in faith to an enormous task (carrying God incarnate in her womb), one of the words used in the modern translation was *whatever.* When I read that word, I knew that it represented an attitude that is an antidote to whining.

> *Mary responded, "I am the Lord's servant. May everything you have said about me come true"* (Luke 1:38 NLT).

In essence she said, "I am willing to accept *whatever* He wants."

So Mama, if you have a bit of a tendency to whine when you are disappointed, consider the impact of your discontented language on your daughter. It would serve you and your daughter well to recognize how you deal with your whining discontentment.

> IT WOULD SERVE YOU AND YOUR DAUGHTER WELL TO RECOGNIZE HOW YOU DEAL WITH YOUR WHINING DISCONTENTMENT.

This was revealed to me readily when I began to ask God to show me my own strategies to try and cure my disappointments. Has your daughter observed you using "mall therapy" as a cure? What about food? Are you inclined to using food as an antidote to your discontent? Behaviors like this model to our girls that shopping or eating can be cures for not getting life on our terms—when in fact, they don't cure anything. These behaviors can actually make our discontentment *worse!*

> *Not that I was ever in need, for I have learned how to get along happily whether I have much or little. I know how to live on almost nothing or with everything. I have learned the secret of living in every situation, whether it be a full stomach or hunger, plenty or want. For I can do everything God asks me to with the help of Christ who gives me the strength and power* (Philippians 4:11-13 TLB).

Many times people quote Philippians 4:13, saying that we can do all things in Christ who strengthens us; but it is rarely quoted in the context of learning to be *content in difficult circumstances* through the help of Christ.

The Greek word for "learned" here refers to a process of being "schooled in" something or being trained. Training can be challenging, but by the power of the Holy Spirit, may we submit to God's training in contentment. This way, we can develop the holy habit of responding to the Lord with a holy *"whatever,"* even in response to disappointing incidents—and we can encourage our daughters to do the same.

My daughter sent me a card while away at college and I have always kept the comment she wrote as a heart treasure for this mama. "I pray that I'll grow up to so love Jesus that no matter what I go through, no matter what season, heartbreak, trial, disillusionment, I'll always trust Jesus like I've seen you do."

The Lord showed me through her remarks that she had been watching me learn contentment when I could have easily whined myself to death. She watched me learn contentment even in the painful aftermath of the suicides of two siblings and the death of my father without Christ.

It's in our suffering that Jesus can teach us that He is *enough*. Learning contentment does not mean expecting changes in our circumstances, but expecting Jesus to be enough in our circumstances. Instead of taking a disappointed teen out for some mall therapy, consider sharing how Jesus was enough in a particularly difficult circumstance in your life.

Too often we parents throw "stuff" at our whining teens rather than helping them grow in contentment. The sooner our daughters learn to let Jesus help them through disappointment, the less vulnerable they will be to seeing boys as anesthesia for their discontented hearts.

> LEARNING CONTENTMENT DOES NOT MEAN EXPECTING CHANGES IN OUR CIRCUMSTANCES, BUT EXPECTING JESUS TO BE ENOUGH IN OUR CIRCUMSTANCES.

Discontentment and Loneliness

The schooling in contentment may require us to pay attention to what we run to in our disappointment. Learning to be content when one is "alone" is a developed skill as well. Some people develop this skill at a younger age because of their circumstances or their personalities. For others, it takes genuine training. Being alone without being lonely means that we must grasp that at this moment God is fully aware of what is going on in our lives; and this moment is in the frame of His plan for us.

> LORD, *you have assigned me my portion and my cup; you have made my lot secure* (Psalms 16:5 NIV).

A dateless Friday night is not a mistake by a loving God. Discontentment, however, flows by focusing on someone else's portion, her date with Mr. Wonderful, and my Friday night with the family again!

> One of the most crucial discoveries I have made over the years, working with and listening to people, is that loneliness has little to do with the absence of people. We can feel lonely in a crowd, among friends, in a marriage, in the family, at a sorority or fraternity house and in a church.[3]

Our loneliness cannot always be fixed, but it can always be accepted as the very will of God *for now;* and acceptance turns it into something beautiful. I witnessed this reality up close and personal observing our daughter spending many Friday nights "alone" but not lonely. She learned the discipline of trusting God with lonely

---

moments. When she was excluded from activities because her friends knew her firm standards, Jessi had the tutorial of trusting God with datelessness as well as exclusion.

> "ONE OF THE MOST CRUCIAL DISCOVERIES I HAVE MADE OVER THE YEARS, WORKING WITH AND LISTENING TO PEOPLE, IS THAT LONELINESS HAS LITTLE TO DO WITH THE ABSENCE OF PEOPLE."[4]

This capacity to be content alone would come to benefit her in the future. When she went off to college alone, without any friends, and then transferred to another college, also without friends there, I knew deep in my heart that this ability to move and thrive among strangers was developed in high school on those lonely Friday nights. We know as moms that even in the most intimate human companionship of marriage, the deepest places of our hearts are only truly satisfied by Jesus.

Jesus cares about our daughters learning to be content. Jesus knows the great gain contentment is in the life of His girls. When your daughter has a dateless Friday night or even a "friendship dateless" one, it is for her a ready tutorial in contentment through the strength of Jesus.

Godliness with contentment is great gain (1 Timothy 6:6 NIV).

I remember being called on a Friday night by the daughter of one of my friends. She was struggling with a dateless and friendless Friday night. After listening to all the painful details, I said to her: "This night is preparation for your future."

I told her that God was preparing her for something in the area of leadership in her future and being able to "handle" disappointing datelessness and absent friends was part of the capacity of a strong leader. In fact, being able to "go it alone" from time to time is actually a *gift to her soul*—a strengthening of her capacity to follow as well as lead.

This young woman went on to become a leader on her college team and an award-winning athlete in college. Today she is a university coach inspiring other girls for the glory of God. She also married an awesome man of God and is a wonderful mother of two precious girls. Helping our teens learn contentment rather than whining over their circumstances has such a profound impact on their future.

Contentment and Unrealistic Expectations

In the letter to the Philippians, Paul writes from prison about a godly contentment that he, himself, had to learn. I believe we can strengthen our understanding of the mystery of contentment by looking at unrealistic expectations that assault our contentment daily.

One day my son shared a quote with me that described this condition precisely. The quote so captured my heart, that I modified it and wrote it on a slip of paper and taped it to the dashboard of my car: "Expectations are pre-meditated resentment."[5]

Throughout that day, as I drove around doing errands, I replayed hundreds of situations from my life where I could clearly trace the expectations that preceded the resentment in my heart. Then I remembered a quote characterizing resentment as "drinking poison and hoping the other person dies."

If my expectations are inextricably linked to premeditated resentment, then I am poisoning myself—unless I immediately commit those expectations to God (see Ps. 62:5). I kept thinking of the holidays, parties, and many social gatherings when my expectations of certain people were so high that it would inevitably spoil the occasion for me. I can't even begin to number the holidays I ruined through my unrealistic expectations of family and friends!

Maybe the next time your teen expresses disappointment in a person or a circumstance it could be a teachable moment to expose her to the "ten versus five" theory. You may be squinting and wondering, "What in the world is the "ten versus five" theory? So glad you asked. It has liberated me and kept joy and contentment in place when circumstances or occasions were far from perfect. Let me explain this wonderful frame you can put around every dream, every event, and every circumstance that you or your daughter will face in the days ahead.

> IF MY EXPECTATIONS ARE INEXTRICABLY LINKED TO PREMEDITATED RESENTMENT, THEN I AM POISONING MYSELF—UNLESS I IMMEDIATELY COMMIT THOSE EXPECTATIONS TO GOD.

Want a "Ten" But Keep Getting a "Five"?

A woman I know went to a professional counselor about her battle with depression. If you looked at this woman's life, you would start screaming, *"How can you possibly be depressed?"* She had it *all;* but having it all had not kept her from constantly struggling with a low-grade fever that ran through her soul.

Finally, she had an epiphany in the counselor's office when she was introduced to the principle of wanting a "'ten' life in a 'five' world." The counselor helped her to see that she wanted something (a "ten" life) that doesn't exist outside the Garden of Eden, where "five" is too often the realistic number. The woman's absurd expectations were fueling her constant trouble with depression.

In various ways, we are all like this woman; we want life to be a "ten." We want to attend family gatherings or go to work every day and never be offended. Hey, we just want to sit at our kitchen tables and not risk getting offended! However, when we learn to expect offenses, we are prepared for days or events that are more "fives" than "tens." If you prepare to go to an event, especially one where you were previously offended or disappointed, and you accept its potential as a "five," but it turns out to be an "eight," then you end up feeling like you've received a bonus.

Exposing your daughter to this principle will be a great enhancement to her growth in contentment, as well as yours. Your daughter has many dreams and many hopes running through her mind daily; this "ten versus five" reality check will help limit the number of shattered dreams ahead of her in the scary tween and teen years.[6]

Discontentment Blinds Us

We, as well as our daughters, are too often consumed with jealousy toward those who have what we have always longed for. This jealousy enhances our discontentment and blinds us to God's blessings in our lives. Encouraging our daughters to see God's blessings and not focus on what is "missing" at this moment is a magnificent mentorship.

A classic example of one woman being jealous of another is the rivalry between the two sisters Leah and Rachel. Ironically, they were both jealous of each other. Leah was jealous because her husband loved Rachel more than he loved her.

> *Jacob lay with Rachel also, and he loved Rachel more than Leah...* (Genesis 29:30 NIV).

Leah spent years trying to win the love of Jacob by having many sons. (Note: It is painful to see too many women who have tried to keep a man's love through the births of children.) Meanwhile, Rachel was jealous of Leah because Leah had a very fertile womb, while Rachel was barren.

The blinding discontentment for Leah resulted from her being so focused on Rachel as the favored wife that she (Leah) couldn't see that she gave birth to the greatest legacy. Here's what I mean: Although Rachel gave birth to Joseph, who would be used by God to save his family during a fierce famine, Leah gave birth to Judah, whose lineage would give birth to Jesus, who would save the *world!* Leah, the invisible one, was given the privilege of bearing a child who would be the forerunner of the Lion of Judah.

All of us have a Rachel in our lives, and are discontent when we compare our lives to hers! The only cure for such discontentment is deeply grasping our own *assigned portion* (see Ps. 16:5). I have this verse on a 4 x 6 card taped up in my bathroom. Daily, I have to choose to resist envying my Rachel, and remain contented in God's assigned portion for me.

DAILY, I HAVE TO CHOOSE TO RESIST "ENVYING MY RACHEL," AND REMAIN CONTENTED IN GOD'S ASSIGNED PORTION FOR ME.

Ask the Lord to reveal to you the "Rachels" who too often send you into discontentment. Remember, for your daughter not to allow jealousy to pickpocket her love for Jesus, she must see this attitude modeled in you.

A relaxed attitude lengthens a man's life; jealousy rots it away (Proverbs 14:30 TLB).

Boy-Craziness: A Common Assault on Contentment

Crushes on boys and boy-craziness are common experiences among tweens (ages ten through twelve) and teens. They are often handled as very innocent matters, not worthy of wasting one's brain cells in worry.

Although boy-craziness seems so innocent, it too often robs precious girls of contentment, and shrinks their capacity for patience in relation to God's script for each life. I came across a list that can help defuse some of the boy-craziness in the lives our young girls. I actually thought the list was great, and you will notice that some of the suggestions have already been shared in previous chapters. I thought the list would be helpful to refresh and add a few additional ideas.

Top Ten List of Ways to Bust Boy-Craziness:

1. Write love letters to God.

2. Create a list of great movies and books that don't fuel impure thoughts and romance.

3. Hang out with friends who aren't boy-crazy.

4. Invest time in the "man in your life"—your dad.

5. Exercise or get involved in sports.

6. Get a mentor to talk to about it.

7. Write a list of your future husband's qualities.

8. Begin a journal to your future husband.

9. Read *Passion and Purity* and *Lady in Waiting*.

10. Go on a mission trip.

I am sure there are other activities to curb this "condition" and restore your daughter's capacity for contentment and patience!

Prep Quiz Question No. 4: What is keeping your teen from doing for others? Is your teen too self-focused? Does she only do for others when it benefits her in the long run?

The preceding list to curb boy-craziness also contains holy habits to help limit whining self-absorption! Before considering whether or not our daughters have pure motives when doing for others, let's take a little heart check ourselves. Here is the simplest question to self-check: How often this week did you do something for someone else without anticipating reciprocation? Reciprocation is not something bad, because mutual reciprocation is often a powerful aspect of a good friendship. The question is more about doing things with a hidden agenda.

Ask yourself the following questions: Why are you doing this? Are you doing it because you know the Lord wants you to do it, or are you doing a particular activity because you are an approval addict? Are you serving because you seek the approval of a certain person?

People-pleasing is a slippery slope. Too many of God's girls have slid down it while trying to scale the unfathomable heights of performance-based acceptance. Contentment does not flow from finally getting the approval of others. Contentment flows from knowing one has already been approved by the King of kings!

> PEOPLE-PLEASING IS A SLIPPERY SLOPE. TOO MANY OF GOD'S GIRLS HAVE SLID DOWN IT WHILE TRYING TO SCALE THE UNFATHOMABLE HEIGHTS OF PERFORMANCE-BASED ACCEPTANCE.

A simple motive check is to ask yourself: "Am I doing this for Jesus or am I doing this so a particular person will admire and applaud my work?" Regular exposure to the truth of God's Word will help expose the motives behind behavior. The Word of God is described as an instrument of God that can discern the motives of one's heart:

For the word of God is alive and powerful. It is sharper than the sharpest two-edged sword, cutting between soul and spirit, between joint and marrow. It exposes our innermost thoughts and desires (Hebrews 4:12 NLT).

Many years ago at a conference in California, the last speaker of the night asked the audience this question: "Do you know what Jesus is going to say the first time He sees you?"

I leaned forward—so far forward I almost fell out of my chair. I didn't want to miss his next statement. Before I could even think about what Jesus might say when He first sees me in heaven, this humble old man said, "Jesus is going to say, 'Do you know how much I have enjoyed living in your body?'"

When I heard that simple sentence, I burst into tears and spent most of the night pondering the question. What a privilege to live in this generation with Jesus possessing my heart and soul. Pray about sharing with your daughter the amazing reality that the King of kings, through the power of His Spirit, is borrowing her body to make a difference for Him while she is on this earth. Such a noble privilege cannot help but enhance one's growth in godliness with contentment which is such great gain! (See First Timothy 6:6.)

Cheering on Discontentment

I have received so many e-mails from "dateless" girls struggling to be content with God's present script for their lives. These girls often describe how other people can enhance their discontentment through the comments they make. Here is just one sample of friends actually "cheering on" discontentment. This young woman lives in the Philippines:

I'm twenty-two years old now and many of my friends have boyfriends, but I don't. I know God is beside me and I'm not alone, but still, I'm tired of being single. It's so hard for me to confess that no man ever loved me. I'm so desperate. No man wants to seek the deepest areas of my heart. Thinking about this always makes me cry. People around me [are] always asking those questions:

1. Don't you have a boyfriend?

2. Have you got a boyfriend?

3. Is there any guy asking you?

4. Don't you want to have a boyfriend?

Those questions always make me sick. But I can't do anything. They don't know that I never had a boyfriend and that makes me so ashamed. I asked God to stop this; I can't be single anymore. I don't want to be alone my whole life.

Not dating at twenty-two years old is not only a formidable problem, but such taunting from friends is terribly challenging to contentment. One of my dearest friends was single for forty years. Part of the reason she could walk such a path was that she had learned the mystery of contentment. She knew that God had not lost her address. She would always respond to "taunting questions" about her prolonged singleness with the fact that this was God's best for her. I would always tell her that her datelessness was her being "spared" painful encounters with Bozo guys!

Moms, let's not encourage our girls to try out for *this* cheerleading squad. We want to spur one another on to good works (see Heb. 10:24 NIV) not cheer one another into more discontentment.

"Don't Waste Brain Cells, Child"

I was reading about a missionary to Pygmies in Africa, who served in difficult circumstances for fifty-two years. How does one persevere in such a challenging environment for that long? This woman's daughter discovered her secret in a diary she had written. In it, the mom had a list of things she refused to do. The list allowed her to be content for fifty-two years in a place that some women wouldn't be content for fifty-two minutes.

Here is Ella's discontentment-buster list:

- Never allow yourself to complain about anything—not even the weather.

- Never picture yourself in any other circumstances or someplace else.

- Never compare your lot with another's. [See Psalms 16.]

- Never allow yourself to wish this or that had been otherwise.

- Never dwell on tomorrow—remember that [tomorrow] is God's, not ours.[7]

As I read this list I can hear my mentor saying, "Child, don't waste good brain cells on what you cannot change." As moms, we need to remind our daughters of these truths, so that they don't waste good brain cells on things they cannot change.

Ella had a list of discontentment-busters. Do you?

A cheerful disposition is good for your health; gloom and doom leave you bone-tired (Proverbs 17:22 MSG).

Don't Feed Discontentment Through Toxic Giving

One last thought about your daughter's discontentment: The culprit is not always her lack of grasping her need for contentment. Sometimes we moms feed our daughters discontentment through "toxic giving."

Let me attempt an explanation. As parents we so want our children to have the best that they never learn to wait for it. Too often, we scurry around trying to secure everything for them, including material things, social situations, and opportunities at school or on the job.

In and of itself, there is nothing wrong with this. As parents, these actions are part of our role. Yet taken to an extreme, they can be very detrimental. We have all seen families go into debt at Christmas because they didn't want their children discontented with their pile under the Christmas tree.

What about the mom who manipulates behind the scenes to make sure her daughter gets onto the cheerleading squad, or arranges for a certain boy to invite her to the prom? All of these more excessive attempts to "give" our girls what we think will make them happy can produce toxic effects.

I read an article recently about "Toxic Charity." The premise just about curled my hair permanently! The writer articulated the progression of toxic giving. I couldn't help but think of this in my own life and in the lives of thousands of parents who have raised very discontented children. These young people live as though they were owed and entitled to the best!

Consider the progression of toxic giving, and its inevitable result, which is discontentment:

1. Give once and you elicit appreciation.

2. Give twice and you create anticipation.

3. Give three times and you create expectation.

4. Give four times and it becomes entitlement.

5. Give five times and you establish dependency.[8]

Too many parents have given so much to their children that the entitlement and dependency does not end after graduation. The next time you have to say no to a purchase for your child or say no to arranging special opportunities for them, just remember the propensity to "toxic giving" and how it can ultimately poison a child with discontentment.

Ruth, the Proverbs 31 Woman, and Contentment

The Book of Ruth is a wonderful profile of a young woman learning contentment in a situation that would naturally produce whining. Because Ruth trusted in the God of Israel, she learned how to be content. Learning to be content produced in her life the very qualities extolled in Proverbs 31.

> BECAUSE RUTH TRUSTED IN THE GOD OF ISRAEL, SHE LEARNED HOW TO BE CONTENT. LEARNING TO BE CONTENT PRODUCED IN HER LIFE THE VERY QUALITIES EXTOLLED IN PROVERBS 31.

One can't help but wonder whether the writer of Proverbs 31 was inspired by Ruth's awesome example. Oral tradition would have passed the inspiring story of Ruth from generation to generation. With Ruth being the great, great, grandmother of King David, it is not a stretch to consider the impact of her story on the writer of Proverbs 31. Consider the following parallels between the woman it describes, and Ruth:

1. Devoted to her family (see Ruth 1:15-18; Prov. 31:10-12,23)

2. Delighted in her work (see Ruth 2:2; Prov. 31:13)

3. Diligent in her labor (see Ruth 2:7,17,23; Prov.31:14-22,24,27)

4. Dedicated to godly speech (see Ruth 2:10,13; Prov. 31:26)

5. Dependent on God (see Ruth 2:12; Prov. 31:30)

6. Dressed with care (see Ruth 3:3; Prov. 31:22,25)

7. Discreet with men (see Ruth 3:6-13; Prov. 31:11-12,23)

8. Delivered blessings (Ruth 4:14-15; Prov. 31:28,29,31)[9]

When I consider how profoundly the Book of Ruth and Proverbs 31 have impacted me as a woman, I have to ask, "Wouldn't the above material be a great little Bible study for you to do with your daughter?" Looking up these verses and examining the character qualities that enhanced Ruth's contentment cannot help but prepare your daughter's heart to be a Young Lady of Contentment.

How awesome to consider sharing this material, not only with your daughter, but also with some of her friends in a little Bible study. The girls could look up the verses and compare them and mark them in their Bibles. Considering the media's taunting challenge of our girls' security and contentment, let these verses from Ruth and Proverbs 31 be a strengthening and restorative exercise!

Chapter 8—Questions for Discussion

1. Would you be described as a contented person or a whiner? How about your daughter? (See First Timothy 6:6.)

2. What tends to suffocate your joy? How about your daughter's joy?

3. Discuss this statement: "Whining is anger squeezed through a tiny hole." Have you ever considered this definition? (See James 4:1-3.)

4. Discuss how whining and/or complaining are contagious (see Phil. 2:14-15; Num. 13:32; 14:1-2; Josh. 14:8). Something to consider: the whining of the ten spies was contagious; but the faith of Joshua and Caleb was not.

5. Did you know the "ten versus five" theory before reading this chapter? Discuss how your expectations rob you of contentment.

6. Discuss the suggestions offered to curb your daughter's crushing on boys.

7. Have you considered creating a No Whining Zone, perhaps in your kitchen area?

8. Have you considered the correlation between a girl's discontentment and her being attracted to a Bozo guy?

9. Are you up for the challenge of sharing the list from Proverbs 31 and Ruth with your daughter and maybe her friends?

10. Discuss Ella's secret list of discontentment busters:

   - Never allow yourself to complain about anything—not even the weather.

   - Never picture yourself in any other circumstances or someplace else.

   - Never compare your lot with another's. [See Psalms 16.]

   - Never allow yourself to wish this or that had been otherwise.

   - Never dwell on tomorrow—remember that [tomorrow] is God's, not ours.[10]

CHAPTER 9

Raising a Young Lady of Conviction

Ruth's Convictions

The Book of Ruth not only tells the story of a Lady in Waiting, but also portrays the profile of a Knight in Shining Armor.

Ruth's choice to wait for God's best resulted in her union with a Boaz rather than a Bozo. Ruth married a man who was a pillar of strength and, moreover, was blessed by the privilege of bearing a son who would be included in the lineage of Jesus Christ.

Ruth's wise choices resulted in her experiencing God's overwhelming goodness.

This honorable young woman did not allow the past influences of a heathen culture to keep her from setting new standards and making wise choices that would honor God. She chose to break her family's sin cycle and establish a new godly cycle.

In Chapter 4 we considered the quality of virtue, the moral excellence that compels us to make prudent choices regarding sexuality. A virtuous wife is characterized in Proverbs 31, and certainly it is our goal as moms to instill virtuous character into our young ladies. In this chapter, I will discuss the *convictions* that undergird virtue.

Conviction, as we know, is a confident belief, and we often speak of it in terms of the confidence of faith—it is my conviction that Jesus Christ has died for my sins. Such faith convictions are then manifested in devotion to God and diligence in serving Him. Just as those actions stem from our faith, the activity of virtue stems from our convictions. It is conviction in the principles of godly standards for dating and marriage that enables us to say *no* when that's required and to say *yes* to God's ways.

A Young Lady of Clear Convictions

Once your daughter begins noticing the boys in her world, it is time to develop the standards that define her convictions. This will enable your daughter to deal daily with what I call the "double-booked" reality of her heart.

Have you ever arrived a bit late for a flight only to find that your seat was given away? Airlines often double-book their seats to ensure they'll fill the plane, especially on popular flights. Likewise, we humans are constantly double-booked between wise and foolish choices.

> ONCE YOUR DAUGHTER BEGINS NOTICING THE BOYS IN HER WORLD, IT IS TIME TO DEVELOP THE STANDARDS THAT DEFINE HER CONVICTIONS.

To use another metaphor, we "hedge our bets," keeping two options open at the same time until we see which one works better or which one comes through. For your daughter to develop discernment about the double-booked condition of her heart is critically important, as her convictions will help her choose wisely between the attention of a Bozo guy and the respect of a Boaz.

Daily your teen will be called to decide whether to rush towards a Bozo (an exploiter of her purity), or wait patiently for a Boaz (a protector of her purity). This double-booked condition is described in Romans 7:15: *"I do not understand what I do. For what I want to do I do not do, but what I hate I do"* (NIV).

The development of clear conviction about the difference between a Bozo and a Boaz will spare your daughter future agony. Ironically, our girls spend so much time getting "ready" for dates—the right outfit, right nail polish, right shoes, right hair accessory—yet spend very little time getting the most critical aspect ready...*their hearts.*

Long before the date, such readiness of heart (conviction) should have determined which guy she was attracted to and going out with in the first place! Here is a simple list of comparisons between a Bozo (see 2 Sam. 13) and a Boaz (see Ruth 2):

1. Bozo is controlled by emotion.

    Boaz controls his emotions. (He may get upset, but knows what to do with it.)

2. Bozo is angered when he doesn't get his way.

    Boaz can rise above disappointment; he knows God will give him peace.

3. Bozo doesn't notice the needs of others. (He might turn it on for you, but don't be impressed unless he does the same for the person across the table.)

    Boaz is courteous and aware, goes the extra mile, and has plenty of room to love lots of people.

4. Bozo is very critical of others, and very intolerant.

    Boaz is tolerant of imperfection because he knows who he is.

5. Bozo is self-centered; he always wants it on his terms (lust thrives in this heart).

    Boaz is other-centered, and therefore self-controlled (lust constrained in this heart).

6. Bozo is rigid and his viewpoint is the only conclusion.

    Boaz is teachable; his heart and mind are open.

7. Bozo always makes excuses for not doing a task well. (If you marry a man like that, you become part of the excuse team.) No one is ever accountable for the way he lives and he always wants sympathy.

   Boaz strives to do his work to the best of his ability and to the glory of Jesus.

8. Bozo lacks integrity; he has no conscience when exploiting a girl's purity.

   Boaz has integrity and is kind, merciful, and gentle. These qualities fuel his protection of a girl's purity.[1]

The Stud Purse

Several years ago, a single woman from New York City sent me a gift. When I first saw it, I was puzzled. Inside the box was a vivid red purse embossed with bright white capital letters spelling out *STUD*. What an odd gift!

Then I read her note and it clarified her intention. Ana had sent me this purse for me to use as a visual aid when teaching teen girls about the local Bozo guys. I began to do just that. On one trip, I found the purse in my suitcase with a glossy brochure melted right onto the purse. I tried in vain to carefully remove the paper that had melted into the plastic, and what remained was a big black mess. I groaned, thinking that my great visual was ruined. But after looking at the black stain for a few moments, the Lord showed me that the stain on my STUD purse was perfect.

You see, the black, messy scar was on the *back* side of the purse, whereas the word *STUD* had not been ruined. So, now I actually had a new and improved visual aid. The next time I used the STUD purse when teaching "How to Avoid a Bozo Guy," I showed the perfect front of the purse, displaying STUD. Then I turned it over and showed the girls the black, messy scar on the back!

When I use this visual, I tell the girls that "STUD guys" too often leave terrible scars on the hearts of girls. The girls go from laughing to groaning as some of them reflect on the Bozo guys who have already hurt their hearts. I now travel with the purse wrapped in tissue paper to protect this poignant visual aid!

For your daughter to avoid marrying a Bozo, she needs to have a clear picture of the difference between God's best—a Boaz—and the all too often "attractive" counterfeit—a Bozo. A Young Lady of Conviction knows the distinct differences between the two. She is not easily distracted by the STUD guys at school. By the way, most girls can give you the name of their school's "stud." This guy is also referred to as a BMOC—Big Man on Campus.

> FOR YOUR DAUGHTER TO AVOID MARRYING A BOZO, SHE NEEDS TO HAVE A CLEAR PICTURE OF THE DIFFERENCE BETWEEN GOD'S BEST—A BOAZ—AND THE ALL TOO OFTEN "ATTRACTIVE" COUNTERFEIT—A BOZO.

Across America, you can find teenage girls swooning whenever a BMOC so much as smiles at them in the hallway en route to his next class. You can hear the girl sharing breathlessly, with her best friend, "he spoke to me after English class!"

This swooning girl is convinced that Mr. BMOC/Stud is interested in her because he spoke to her for almost a whole minute. But let's be sober here! The problem with BMOCs is how they can potentially scar our girls. When a girl is in awe of a guy like this, she is more vulnerable to being taken advantage of physically. The stud knows that she is "swooning and crushing" on him, and he is more than willing to give her the attention she is hungry for—which often results in the swooning team being escorted to the No Zone by the BMOC. This may seem cruel or even exaggerated, but Mom, I have been listening for four decades to teen girls who have been taken advantage of, used, and disposed of like paper cups.

No Bozo Pajamas

In 1984 I was scheduled to speak at a singles' event. The topic was "How to Avoid a Bozo." The single gal hosting the event decided to have T-shirts made with a classic No Bozo sign on the front. That T-shirt became my favorite display of my heart's message for all single daughters of the King. In fact, I was so committed to my daughter avoiding a Bozo in a life mate, that when she was only four years old, once a week at least, I would have her sleep in this No Bozo T-shirt. The funny thing was that little Jessi "hated" that shirt for some reason. But I would tell her, "Well, sweetheart, I hate Bozos and I love you," and proceed to pull the shirt over her head.

I now travel all over using the aged No Bozo T-shirt as a visual. Unlike my four-year-old, people squeal with delight when they see it. The STUD purse and the No Bozo T-shirt communicate my passionate agenda of spreading the word: *No Bozos* for our girls! (In fact, my husband ordered me Florida vanity plates with the words *No Bozo*. My passion is now displayed on my car, everywhere I go!!)

Mentored by Hollywood

I may seem to some like an extremist mom, but I was simply committed as a mama to do everything in my power to guard my daughter's heart and keep her from being exploited by some Bozo guy.

I am convinced that the Bozo tribe has increased the past few decades due to the breakup of homes and parents working too much. One can't help but consider how few fathers are mentoring their boys in the qualities of honor and purity. Instead, boys as well as girls are being babysat and even mentored *by Hollywood*. This is how they are learning about the opposite sex. No wonder there are so many relational crimes being committed among even teenagers. These offenses include emotional and sexual bullying, date rape, drugging rape...and the horrifying list goes on.

Let's have no doubt about this. Hollywood has accelerated the exploitation of girls. When a boy is rude and hurtful to a girl, too often she thinks he is "just being a guy." Girls have watched hours of TV where teen boys act foolishly and hurtfully. The girls assume this is no more than teen masculinity. They don't even know there's something better.

Is this a hopeless situation? Are all boys destined to be Bozo guys? I am not willing to give in to this idea; I firmly believe that part of the answer is exposing Bozo guys to girls who actually have godly standards. Girls who act like princesses from an unshakable Kingdom (not the entitled, selfish kind of "princess") can make a powerful impact on the guys around them, whether at school or youth group. Our daughters can set standards that Hollywood has long since abandoned, which will help them resist being

Bozo bait. Girls who are internally beautiful and are ladies of conviction can profoundly impact their world.

Listen to what the second President of the United States, John Adams, once said:

> From all that I have read of history and government, of human life and manner, I have drawn this conclusion—the manners of women were the most infallible barometer to ascertain the degree of morality and virtue of a nation.[2]

Of course we want the boys to act like young men of honor, but until they have that tutorial, our daughters can be strengthened in the growth of their own convictions. Clear convictions give our daughters the courage to say no when a boy tries to escort her to the No Zone. Girls who know how to say *no* are actually helping the boys to grow up! Recall this quote from a best-selling author described the gift of *no:*

> Women saying no to men, not letting men have sex with them, causes men to step up....I think men need women to be women, and we need to be made to jump through some hoops. If a woman withholds sex until she gets what *she* wants, we are all better for it.[3]

For some girls, saying no will be like learning a foreign language. However, a clear understanding of what Mr. Right and Mr. Wrong are like will help girls comprehend that "foreign" word. When girls can differentiate between Prince Charming and Prince Harming, they will be more confident in saying no—a *no* that they will use when invited out by Bozo guys!

WHEN GIRLS CAN DIFFERENTIATE BETWEEN PRINCE CHARMING AND PRINCE HARMING, THEY WILL BE MORE CONFIDENT IN SAYING NO.

Most Significant List on an iPhone

Prep Quiz Question No. 15: Does your teen carry (in her wallet or on her cell phone) a list of the qualities that describe Mr. Right?

When my niece was a young teen, she was challenged by her youth leader to make a list describing an ideal guy and put it in her wallet. She wrote out her list of what she felt was God's best. My niece carried this list throughout high school and college and went on to marry Mr. Wonderful. (Nowadays, teen girls can carry "the list" on their phones.)

The great wisdom in such a practice is that young girls need to decide in advance what a man worth waiting for is like. You don't decide in the moment when you're crushing on a guy. You decide in advance—before the emotional tsunami hits.

Years after my niece showed me her list, I met a girl who had just graduated from Auburn University. She also had a list describing the ideal guy. At the time I met this young woman my husband worked in a mission organization where an adorable single guy was serving. This guy was everyone's crush. He was as wonderful inside as he was outside. I constantly heard remarks about him from several young, single women.

One day I asked the girl from Auburn to share with me a few of the descriptive statements from her "Mr. Right" list. As she shared them, I couldn't help but think of the adorable single guy who served with my husband.

Here is what was on her list:

1. Spirit-controlled Christian

2. Jesus #1 in his life, not just an ornament

3. Broken: understands how to rely totally upon Jesus

4. Ministry-minded: wherever he is, he is available

5. Motivator: a man of vision, concerned about lost souls

6. Sensitive spirit: in tune to the needs of others

7. Understands the awesome responsibility of a husband to his wife

8. Humble enough to be a disciple (teachable) and able to disciple others

9. Man of prayer: knows the key to success is his private time with God

10. Family man: desires to have children and raise them properly for God's glory[4]

You may have guessed this by now, but the young woman from Auburn ended up dating the wonderful young man who worked with my husband. Not only did they date, but they married—and they have been happily married for almost two decades. Annually, when I receive their Christmas card, I think of the girl with the list of her ideal guy. Her list helped her say no to Bozo guys, and it clarified when her Mr. Right needed a *yes* from her.

The above list may seem utterly impossible to consider in the 21st century, but I think it is a great list to inspire you to pray for such a man for your daughter. You may not have had a list or such conviction when you were a teen or even in college; but that doesn't mean the list isn't applicable for your daughter.

In 2007, I was getting ready to write another book and I decided to send out a questionnaire to a few hundred guys I knew. (Having worked with professional athletes for fifteen years at that time, I knew a lot of guys.) The responses I received were so touching and inspiring. One of my conclusions after reading them was this: Deep in their hearts men know God's ideals. They have the desire to be better guys, not Bozo guys. Guys need girls who have standards and convictions to remind them of those ideals deep in their hearts.

Since they show that the requirement of the law are written on their hearts, their consciences also bearing witness, and their thoughts now accusing, now even defending them (Romans 2:15 NIV).

A Young Lady of Conviction can be a gentle but strong reminder of the God-given conscience that nudges young men to stop acting like Bozos.

While waiting for my time to speak for FCA at the University of South Carolina, a young man approached me. With the biggest smile, he said, "I just want you to know that I read your book."

My stunned reply was, "Really? You read *Lady in Waiting*?"

"Yes ma'am, I have," he stated. "When my girlfriend broke up with me, she handed me *Lady in Waiting* and said 'This is why I'm breaking up with you.'"

He went on to tell me how mad and in shock he was as he returned to his dorm room and threw down the book. Later on, and somewhat calmed down, he picked up the book and started to read it, out of curiosity. Then he said to me, "You know what the best part about reading that book was? Now I know what a *woman* worth waiting for is like."

His final words to me put a huge smile on my face. That was when he said, "All the guys in my suite also read it."

> A YOUNG LADY OF CONVICTION CAN BE A GENTLE BUT STRONG REMINDER OF THE GOD-GIVEN CONSCIENCE THAT NUDGES YOUNG MEN TO STOP ACTING LIKE BOZOS.

Whether they are guys or girls, all of our children deserve to be exposed to the character qualities of truth, purity, patience, contentment, security, devotion, faith, and a passionate pursuit of Christ. It's imperative that our girls be exposed to them early enough so that their young hearts will be given a heart guard. I meet girls all the time who say, "My youth pastor took us through *Lady in Waiting*, but when I got to college and met so many Bozo guys, I called home and asked my mom to send my copy of the book—for a major refresher course!"

So they revisit it again. It is a huge blessing of my life that, more times than I can count, college students have shown me their shabby copies of *Lady in Waiting* (including broken, taped-up bindings). It has become their guidebook through the Bozo minefields.

Superficiality of Appearance

Growing up, I noticed that I was always attracted to guys with dark hair and dark eyes; whereas I had friends who were attracted to guys with blonde hair and blue eyes. These attractions were a reflection of not only our personal preferences but also a level of immaturity. The ideal guy each of us had in mind was external; the idea was limited to his physical charac-teristics. Whenever I hear girls describing guys as being so cute or so hot, I always ask, "What is his heart like? How does he treat those around him?" God's Word speaks loudly to the superficiality of appearance.

> *But the LORD said to Samuel, "Do not consider his appearance or his height, for I have rejected him. The LORD does not look at the things man looks at. Man looks at the outward appearance, but the LORD looks at the heart" (1 Samuel 16:7 NIV).*

When my husband and I first met, he was *not* struck with love at first sight. In fact, his first thought was, "What in the world just walked into the Bible study!" I had just moved to South Florida from California. I looked like the wildest hippie, with my very short dress and wire-rimmed glasses, long crazy hair, and the biggest Bible ever carried to a youth meeting!

My first thought when I saw my husband was, "This can't be the youth leader. He must be the pastor!" My husband's hair was very short and he was all dressed up, wearing a tie, and leading the youth Bible study. My youth leader in California didn't own a tie and had long hair. If my husband and I had made our future decisions about each other based on appearance, we would not have married. He was blonde and blue-eyed—the opposite of what I normally was attracted to. I had dark hair and dark eyes—the opposite of his high school sweetheart.

WHENEVER I HEAR GIRLS DESCRIBING GUYS AS BEING SO CUTE OR SO HOT, I ALWAYS ASK, "WHAT IS HIS HEART LIKE? HOW DOES HE TREAT THOSE AROUND HIM?"

Every young woman needs to confront her stereotypical view of what is ideal in a guy. Here's why:

Too many single women have missed wonderful treasures in godly guys because the treasure was not encased in a B.B.B. [bronzed, blue-eyed blonde] or T.D.H. [tall, dark, and handsome]. The Lord will probably not require you to date a guy who repulses you physically. But you need to be open to guys who do not fit your desired stereotype. Too often a guy may satisfy your eyesight, but leave your heart empty and still longing.[5]

As a mom, you are the first schoolteacher for your child. Look for occasions when you can guide your child toward the heart of a person and away from the superficiality of appearance.

Whenever our children would describe others as being "cute" or "hot," I would ask questions: "Are they kind? Do they love others? Are they generous? Are they giving?" I helped them to look past the surface to the heart issues that were the *real* issue.

Prep Quiz Question No. 7: Does your daughter know that girls play at sex to get love, and boys play at love to get sex?

In reply to this prep quiz question, I want to share a ghastly but sobering story that impacted me so deeply that it needs to be shared with every single teen girl I encounter. First, they need to grasp this reality: a boy doesn't treat a girl with special deference just because he claims to "love" her. A boy's special treatment of a particular girl is part of his hormone-throbbing agenda. He is (whether consciously or subconsciously) on the hunt for a girl who will join him in the adventure of exploring the No Zone!

Just as boys are addicted to sports and video games, they are also driven by the Number One need of *all* males—*sex!* This is in their wiring, and this hyped-up sexual society has not encouraged them to bulk up the muscle of self-control!

So here is the *must share* story that I saw on *Oprah* one day. Two teenagers, a boy and girl, and their mothers were guests on the show. These teens were willing to discuss on TV their "being ready to have intercourse." Now, the couple had dated almost a year, beginning at age fourteen. During that time they had progressed through the No Zone, and now felt their love justified their readiness to go "all the way."

The two mothers voiced their opinions. One mother was appalled at the suggestion and the other mother felt it was the natural progression of love. The teens continued to defend what they "felt" about each other and how their love made intercourse seem so right.

Besides the million-plus TV viewers listening to the teens, there was an expert sex therapist on the show. I couldn't wait to hear what this "expert" would say in response. I was literally on the edge of my seat.

The doctor leaned forward and directed her question to the young boy. "After you two finally have sex, how long will you continue to date your girlfriend?"

In the brief moment before the boy replied, the camera shifted to his girlfriend, showing her adoring gaze toward him. She obviously anticipated his loving reply. Yet without another moment of hesitation, the boy said, "Maybe six more months."

Of course, the camera caught the shock on the girl's face. The wise doctor immediately directed her next question to the girl: "Did his answer surprise you?"

"Yes!" the poor girl replied, clearly stunned. "I thought because we love each other our love is forever."

This fifteen-year-old girl did not know the hard truth that "guys play at love to get sex." Then the doctor asked the girl, "Are you now reconsidering going all the way with him?"

The teen girl quickly replied, "Yes, I am reconsidering."

Her reply brought a huge round of applause from the audience. And I sat in my front room screaming: "Don't do it, girlfriend. Sex is not love!"

There is a heartbreaking story in God's Word (see 2 Sam. 13:1-16) where a prince declared his love for a particular virgin named Tamar. He actually stated that he was "lovesick" for her. (Note: love does not make you sick—crushing and lusting make you sick!) After Prince Amnon got what he wanted sexually, by raping this innocent girl, the Scripture recounts a most painful outcome:

> *Then Amnon hated her with intense hatred. In fact, he hated her more than he had loved her. Amnon said, "Get up and get out!"* (2 Samuel 13:15 NIV)

I can say with certainty that most of our girls will never face something as horrendous as rape, but I can also say that plenty of our girls will encounter guys who would attempt to seduce them with words. This seduction terminology needs to be exposed. Some of the most common lines Bozo guys use are: "I have never felt this way about anybody," or, "You're different than any other girl in our school/youth group."

Older guys consistently utilize these ploys to seduce younger girls who are vulnerable to such flattery!

LOVE DOES NOT MAKE YOU SICK—CRUSHING AND LUSTING MAKE YOU SICK!

Fire Wall of Prayer Around Our Girls

One of the worst aspects of the story about Amnon's rape of Tamar is to find out that his Hebrew name, *Amnon,* means "trustworthy." He's a prince who certainly did not live his up to his name. And Mom, I want you to know something: Your girls are around boys at church who are Christians, but they don't live up to their names, either. They are indeed princes related to the King of kings, but they bring dishonor to that name. I say to parents all the time, "Pray about the Amnons who prey among our kids, who come into our youth groups, who are in our schools."

MOM, I WANT YOU TO KNOW SOMETHING: YOUR GIRLS ARE AROUND BOYS AT CHURCH WHO ARE CHRISTIANS, BUT THEY DON'T LIVE UP TO THEIR NAMES.

I used to pray and even fast about a "prince" in our daughter's class at school whom I knew was crazy about her. I knew he was a prince who was not living up to his name. No matter how charming he attempted to be—especially around me—I knew he was a Bozo. My husband knew this young man, too, and he would often pray with me for our daughter, repeating the same request: "God protect our daughter from this Bozo guy!" Our prayers were answered and our daughter is happily married to a young pastor.

Prep Quiz Question No. 11: Do you know why so many precious girls marry Bozo guys? Did you know that sex blinds a girl to the Bozo she is dating or attracted to?

I know kids who were raised in fabulous homes with very attentive parents, parents who have sacrificed so much for their girls. Yet these precious girls still end up dating loser guys. How is this possible?

Whenever I hear such a description, I know this girl has become involved physically with her boyfriend. I say that confidently because I have seen it time and time again. Let me illustrate with an example of this "blinding" reality.

One year our church hosted a doubles tennis tournament for young singles. This one couple got up to the net and the girl missed the first ball. Then she missed the next serve. Her boyfriend and tennis partner completely lost it and got so upset he threw the tennis racket at her!

Well, all the people who saw this incident were stunned. They were sure this couple would not be dating by the end of the day. Several girls said to me, "I bet she's breaking up with him tonight."

The next day, the couple strolled into Sunday school class, hand in hand. After class several of the girls confronted me with this question: "Mrs. Kendall, how is she still dating a guy who got so furious and threw a tennis racket at her?"

My immediate reply, "It's because they're having sex. The girls gasped, and another question burst out of their mouths.

"How can you say that, Mrs. Kendall?"

My reply to their second question was simple: "Sex is blinding. When you disobey God's design for sex, the built-in consequence is blindness to the Bozo you are dating."

It's a heartbreaking irony that wonderful Christian kids who have floated around in the pool of God's grace for years assume that they can disobey God's clear standards for moral purity and escape any consequences. Many a Christian girl has assumed that her "love" for a guy is a free pass for disobeying God's standards. She is not even aware that her disobedience is like a choke chain around her neck. It strangles her emotionally and spiritually. She becomes more and more uptight with her parents. Lying becomes her second language—lying that enables her to sneak off on clandestine trips to the No Zone.

> IT'S A HEARTBREAKING IRONY THAT WONDERFUL CHRISTIAN KIDS WHO HAVE FLOATED AROUND IN THE POOL OF GOD'S GRACE FOR YEARS ASSUME THAT THEY CAN DISOBEY GOD'S CLEAR STANDARDS FOR MORAL PURITY AND ESCAPE ANY CONSEQUENCES.

I know that such stories are painful to face—whether your daughter is young enough that you cannot imagine such things, or just old enough to have hit some rough patches. But let me say this loud and clear: It is always a *good thing* to be alert, even to the most troubling realities. Only our sober awareness as parents and our commitment to praying for our daughters and their friends will lead us to do the work of instilling rock-solid convictions in them from a young age.

As you likely already know, moms, in the culture we now live in, such convictions do not develop spontaneously; they must be taught and encouraged and enforced in all the creative ways God gives you to do so.

I am cheering you on from afar!

Chapter 9—Questions for Discussion

1. Does your teen carry a list of the qualities of Mr. Right in her wallet or on her cell phone?

2. Does the following list (with added references) seem too extensive or too idealistic for the 21st century? Why or why not?

   a. Spirit-controlled Christian (see Eph. 5:18)

   b. Jesus #1 in his life, not just an ornament (see Mark 12:30)

   c. Broken: understands how to rely totally upon Jesus (see Phil. 4:13)

    d. Ministry-minded: wherever he is, he is available (see 1 Cor. 4:2)

    e. Motivator: a man of vision, concerned about lost souls (see Rom. 10:14)

    f. Sensitive spirit: in tune to the needs of others (see Gal. 6:2)

    g. Understands the awesome responsibility of a husband to his wife (see Eph. 5:25-31)

    h. Humble enough to be a disciple (teachable) and able to disciple others (see Matt. 28:19-20)

    i. Man of prayer: knows the key to success is his private time with God (see Col. 4:2)

    j. Family man: desires to have children and raise them properly for God's glory (see Prov. 22:6)[6]

3. Have you taught your daughter about the superficiality of appearance? (See First Samuel 16:7.)

4. Does your daughter know that girls play at sex to get love, and boys play at love to get sex?

5. Discuss the *Oprah* show illustration of the teens who thought they were ready for sex.

6. Do you know why so many precious girls marry Bozo guys? Did you know that sex blinds a girl to the Bozo she's dating? Explain.

7. Discuss how premarital sex blinds a girl to the Bozo she is dating (see Gal. 6:7-8).

8. Review and discuss the list comparing Bozos and Boazes (found near the beginning of this chapter). Reflect on the Bozo qualities revealed in Second Samuel 13, and the Boaz qualities seen in Ruth 2.

For Additional Study...

Women are well acquainted with the "ideal woman" chapter, Proverbs 31. Very few know about the "ideal man" chapter excerpted verse by verse, below.

Ruth 2:1-16 (NIV)

1. *Now Naomi had a relative on her husband's side, from the clan of Elimelech, a man of standing, whose name was Boaz.*

2. *And Ruth the Moabitess said to Naomi, "Let me go to the fields and pick up the left-over grain behind anyone in whose eyes I find favor." Naomi said to her, "Go ahead, my daughter."*

3. *So she went out and began to glean in the fields behind the harvesters. As it turned out, she found herself working in a field belonging to Boaz, who was from the clan of Elimelech.*

4. *Just then Boaz arrived from Bethlehem and greeted the harvesters, "The LORD be with you!" "The LORD bless you!" they called back.*

5. *Boaz asked the foreman of his harvesters, "Whose young woman is that?"*

6. *The foreman replied, "She is the Moabitess who came back from Moab with Naomi.*

7. *"She said, 'Please let me glean and gather among the sheaves behind the harvesters.' She went into the field and has worked steadily from morning till now, except for a short rest in the shelter."*

8. *So Boaz said to Ruth, "My daughter, listen to me. Don't go and glean in another field and don't go away from here. Stay here with my servant girls.*

9. *"Watch the field where the men are harvesting, and follow along after the girls. I have told the men not to touch you. And whenever you are thirsty, go and get a drink from the water jars the men have filled."*

10. *At this, she bowed down with her face to the ground. She exclaimed, "Why have I found such favor in your eyes that you notice me—a foreigner?"*

11. *Boaz replied, "I've been told all about what you have done for your mother-in-law since the death of your husband—how you left your father and mother and your homeland and came to live with a people you did not know before.*

12. *"May the LORD repay you for what you have done. May you be richly rewarded by the LORD, the God of Israel, under whose wings you have come to take refuge."*

13. *"May I continue to find favor in your eyes, my lord," she said. You have given me comfort and have spoken kindly to your servant— though I do not have the standing of one of your servant girls."*

14. *At mealtime Boaz said to her, "Come over here. Have some bread and dip it in the wine vinegar." When she sat down with the harvesters, he offered her some roasted grain. She ate all she wanted and had some left over.*

15. *As she got up to glean, Boaz gave orders to his men, "Even if she gathers among the sheaves, don't embarrass her.*

16. *"Rather, pull out some stalks for her from the bundles and leave them for her to pick up, and don't rebuke her."*

After studying this chapter, consider reading the contrasting "Bozo" chapter: Second Samuel 13:1-16.

Raising a Young Lady of Patience

Ruth's Patience

Ruth was a wonderful example of patience. She did not allow her circumstances or lack of male companionship to cause her to be impatient. Instead, she concentrated on developing companionship with her heavenly Father, and chose to let Him bring her a husband as He saw fit.

Concern over the ticking of her "biological clock" did not make her fearful of the future. Moving to a new country amongst hostile people did not make her fearful, either. Instead she concentrated, not on getting a man, but on following the Lord and being a lady of character.

We can infer from what the Bible tells us of Ruth's faith-filled behavior that she took one day at a time, knowing that God was not bound by her circumstances or her age. And through the process, she used the waiting time to become the woman God wanted her to be.

My heart's passion is twofold: for all of God's girls to wait for His best; and for me to be used as His instrument to encourage their waiting, whether it be for a husband and family, a vocation, or any other calling of God.

My heart breaks when I encounter again and again the epidemic impatience His daughters show in waiting on Him. One evening years ago I wrote a poem in response to yet another young woman ending up with yet another Bozo guy. She ended up with him because she became impatient with God's script for her life.

This simple verse is a glimpse at my heart's cry:

Don't Settle

I hope you don't consider me to meddle,
When I say don't settle.
Have you heard my heart scream?
Don't give up your dream.
So many have settled for Prince Harming,
Rather than courageously wait for Prince Charming.
Settling for a Bozo,
Whose heart will be a no show.
Despairing over your absent knight in shining armor,
Will escort you into the arms of a carnival charmer.
Your Designer has dreamed much better for you,
Don't settle for a man who can't love you through and through.

Prep Quiz Question No. 17: How patient is your teen?

Teaching our children how to postpone present pleasures for future fulfillment is a concept that is familiar to most of us. Yet it is less frequently practiced in our more recent "fast food," "instant access" generations.

In an article about child rearing in France, the author expounds on practices that are generations old and that seem to aid in raising children who are "calm and resilient." The article states:

One of the keys to this education is the simple act of learning how to wait. It is why the French babies I meet mostly sleep through the night from two or three months old. Their parents don't pick them up the second they start crying, allowing the babies to learn how to fall back asleep. It is also why French toddlers will sit happily at a restaurant. Rather than snacking all day like American children, they mostly have to wait until mealtime to eat. (French kids consistently have three meals a day and one snack around 4 p.m.)...

Could it be that teaching children how to delay gratification—as middle-class French parents do—actually makes them calmer and more resilient? Might this partly explain why middle-class American kids, who are in general more used to getting what they want right away, so often fall apart under stress?[1] (emphasis added)

The author interviewed a labor lawyer who is also a mom and asked about the process of teaching her kids patience. Her reply was captivating, explaining that "her family's daily rituals are an ongoing apprenticeship in how to delay gratification."[2]

What an important reminder that our home life is an apprenticeship for either patience or impatience and for selflessness or selfishness. Have you enrolled your daughter in the apprenticeship of patience? Do you know that you can consider every setback and every closed door your daughter encounters as part of this critical apprenticeship?

The next time your daughter impatiently taps her foot, you can make it a teachable moment—even if it means she has to wait *longer*—so that the apprenticeship in patience can have an honor-roll graduate.

Is *Wait* a Cuss Word?

The apprenticeship of patience is not an option for our children's security and happiness. Our children's having to *wait* for things they really want develops their self-control. This will bless absolutely every aspect of their future. A parenting pattern of instant gratification for whatever a child wants will undermine the child's chance to become patient.

Is the four-letter word *wait* like a cuss word to your teen? Whenever I speak to a teen gathering and mention this four-letter word *wait,* I always hear sighing and groaning from the girls. Would your daughter be one of the teens groaning in the audience? How patient is your teen?

Waiting is a prerequisite for God's best. And if God's best is a husband, then waiting on God is the best plan for your daughter finding a Boaz. Conversely, impatience is the easiest way to find a Bozo. Even if the young girls I speak to think of waiting as a "harsh requirement," I ask them this question: "What is worse than waiting?"

As the girls ponder their answers, I blurt out my answer: "Wishing you had!" I have spent decades counseling all those who *wished* they had waited for their Boaz.

Since ancient times no one has heard, no ear has perceived, no eye has seen any God besides you, who acts on behalf of those who **wait** *for Him* (Isaiah 64:4 NIV).

Vulnerability to Missionary Dating

Patience was the red carpet that Ruth walked down to receive God's best for her: Boaz, a man worth waiting for. I am sad to report that I have seen thousands of precious girls miss the red carpet to God's best because of their inability to wait. Impatience in everyday life may seem like a minor flaw in your daughter, but patience is critical for her to receive God's best—a Boaz instead of a counterfeit...a Bozo.

What challenges us moms now more than ever is the fact that the pressure for dating and "romantic" interactions with boys begins at younger and younger ages. Crushes and peer pressure that may have begun in sixth or seventh grade a generation ago now occur in third or fourth grades. By the time a girl is in high school and allowed to go out on dates, she has been immersed in a boy-crazy, sexually-saturated culture for years! At that point, the longer she is dateless, the more vulnerable she becomes to impatience in waiting for "Mr. Right."

I will go into many different principles to aid moms in navigating this prolonged era of singleness in their daughters' lives; but one, critical pitfall I will begin with here is what we call "missionary dating."

Dating was never meant to be a mission field; but many a young (and not-so-young) Christian woman is tempted to venture into that perilous field. I have received so many letters from single girls who want to know if it is OK to date a nonbeliever. They defend the guy they are interested in by describing how wonderful he is. They write pages of biographical description of this "Mr. Right" and conclude with something like, "Well, the only fault I can find in him at this time is that he is not a Christian!"

If at that moment I could Skype this girl, the only sound she would hear would be a screaming Mimi over the Internet! Here is one of the replies I sent to a young girl who was defending her "religious" boyfriend.

Dear K_____:

FASTEN YOUR SEATBELT...I care too much about you to not share the truth.

How ironic that you went to a secular college to be a witness for Jesus and now you are missionary dating. The key is not how nice your boyfriend is or how polite or how charming or unselfish or hardworking he is. There are thousands of religious people that have the same qualities. BOAZ had all these qualities, but he had the most differentiating one: he loved the LORD and the WORD, and LIVED IT.

You said, "He is perfect for me, except for his lack of relationship with Jesus. Girlfriend, his relationship with JESUS IS ALL THAT MATTERS! The key is your boyfriend's love for Jesus, not his devotion to you. You know the difference and you know that you are disobeying God's Word in Second Corinthians 6:14 and Amos 3:3. The reality is you are looking for permission to love someone who is charming but is not born again. You even admitted your fear of not finishing the race. Well, girlfriend, you are not running in your lane. You have already chosen your boyfriend over Jesus. That is why your friends have been trying to warn you to guard your heart.

The honorable thing would be for you to stop dating this guy because he isn't born again. And he won't be born again by dating you, because you have accepted him as a charming nonbeliever, so WHY SHOULD HE CHANGE?! Have you ever considered the reality that YOU ARE STANDING in the way of his coming to Jesus because you have "fogged up" the window of witness!?

If you REALLY LOVE JESUS, you wouldn't want to date a guy who isn't going to be a thriving, growing member of TEAM JESUS. Your nice guy isn't even on TEAM JESUS.

No sooner did I e-mail the above reply, that I received another e-mail:

Hi Jackie,

Please could you help me? I am in love with an unbeliever. I have been for four years. Although he has asked me to date him I have told him what I believe, that it is not right for me to date an unbeliever. I really don't want to. I want to please God with all my heart. I have been praying for him to come to know Jesus but he hasn't changed. I feel like God has told me he will get saved but I don't know when; it could be years and years. There is another guy who likes me who is a Christian but I don't know him very well. I would like to give him a chance because he seems really nice, is involved in his church, and loves God. I just don't want to have feelings toward this other non-Christian guy because I know they will influence me. Please help me!

Sometimes I just want to cry because so many of God's girls are impatiently settling for guys who aren't growing Christians. As I grieve over so many of the e-mails I receive daily, I am reminded that *who* a girl loves is a "billboard" of her heart's condition spiritually. Girls who settle for Bozo guys or even very nice nonbelievers are displaying to the world their impatient hearts. Me-centric girls do not know how to be patient, and their appetite for instant gratification often results in vulnerability to Bozo guys!

Prep Quiz Question No. 14: Do you know how to be a "spiritual monitor" of your daughters "crushing" on guys?

Now let's back up a bit to what goes on before a girl gets herself embroiled in a relationship with a non-Christian. Long before such an attachment was formed, this young woman began noticing boys. Girls notice boys. This is a normal experience. For a girl to begin to focus and think about the boy she has noticed is not unusual. What you daughter needs most from you when she mentions a cute guy at school is for you to first *listen*.

Sometimes one of your daughter's friends will mention a cute guy at school. As you continue to listen to your daughter and her friend, look for an opportunity to ask the girls what they like most about this particular guy. Ask for reasons why this guy stands out among all the other boys. Take note if their descriptions are all externals: hair, eyes, smile, height, and even a cool car!

When they have finished their external descriptions of the "cool guy" they are crushing on, ask them to tell you something about how he acts and how he treats others. Listen for character qualities that enhance his cute smile. Every daughter needs a spiritual monitor, even when they are just crushing on boys—one who will listen and ask wise questions and give input *after* plenty of listening.

I have a friend who came home from a date and was so excited she was talking a hundred miles an hour to her mother about this wonderful guy and the perfect evening that they had together. Her mother was a wise woman and a spiritual monitor for her two daughters. Her reply to her daughter's enthusiastic rant was, "Kimmy, sweetie, you need to reign that in a little bit. Don't go buy a bride's magazine. Don't already name your children. You've had one date, OK?"

Now her Mom's reply may seem extreme, but girls and women alike move fast in the area of emotional attachments. A precious teen who's had one date with a guy is already dreaming about going to the senior prom with him—and they are both only freshmen.

Maybe you're thinking, "Are you kidding me?" But some of you know what I am talking about. I had a crush on a guy in fifth grade, and I constantly wrote my first name and his last name on my school folder—Jackie Burke! I know this seems silly, but those silly little crushes morph into bigger crushes. Too often, without a spiritual monitor in a mom, a girl can get herself into some emotional as well as physical trouble.

> GIRLS AND WOMEN ALIKE MOVE FAST IN THE AREA OF EMOTIONAL ATTACHMENTS. A PRECIOUS TEEN WHO'S HAD ONE DATE WITH A GUY IS ALREADY DREAMING ABOUT GOING TO THE SENIOR PROM WITH HIM—AND THEY ARE BOTH ONLY FRESHMEN.

A spiritual monitor is like a governor on a gas pedal. It protects the driver of the "love mobile" from speeding into the arms of a Bozo. Having time to listen to our girls and share their joys and dreams is critical during the tween and teen years. Your input shouldn't be preachy, but kind. Listen actively and with genuine curiosity to study your child's heart.

Too often our girls can't hear us because our voice tones make our wisdom sound like noise! Our daughter dated a couple of wonderful Christian guys, and I struggled to not be an overbearing cheerleader for the guy of my choosing. I would pray constantly and listen as much as I prayed. Only in desperate moments did I weigh in verbally. Being a spiritual monitor takes much prayer and wisdom.

I believe the freshmen girls in our lives, whether they're freshmen in high school or freshmen in college, need spiritual monitors. So many of the girls that I "love on" each year at Palm Beach Atlantic University are still in need of spiritual monitors, even when they are no longer living at home. They need reminders of the truths that their moms shared with them while in junior and senior high school.

He who walks with wise men will be wise, but the companion of fools will suffer harm (Proverbs 13:20).

Enhanced Heartbreak

Just recently a dear girl who was raised with an incredible spiritual legacy was deeply hurt during a breakup with an awesome Christian guy. As I listened to the details of their dating relationship I clearly heard— *"no spiritual monitor."*

This precious girl did not have anyone cautioning her not to outrun what God intended for this dating relationship. They were discussing marriage early in their dating journey. Everyone around them talked about them being the perfect couple. Now, this all may seem pretty innocent, but honestly it was premature enthusiasm and assumption on the part of all the "older people" commenting on the couple's dating.

The encouragement of a spiritual monitor would have helped this young woman enact what I call the "Eleventh Commandment:" *Thou shalt not defraud thyself.*

Running ahead of where a relationship actually is, emotionally or even logistically, readily leads to one or both people suffering from a defrauding of their own making.

I have spent three decades listening to "enhanced heartbreak" flowing from the hearts of girls who do not have spiritual monitors in their lives. These girls only had the cheering crowds that would end up stunned when the "perfect couple" broke up. The cheering crowds do not do a good job comforting heartbroken girls; and they don't realize they were part of the problem in the first place. Cheering with caution is the best thing any friend or parent can do for a friend or daughter who is dating.

> CHEERING WITH CAUTION IS THE BEST THING ANY FRIEND OR PARENT CAN DO FOR A FRIEND OR DAUGHTER WHO IS DATING.

James 4 has a wonderful reminder for all of us concerning our dreamy ideas and runaway feelings:

Now listen, you who say, ["I know this is the one for me" or], *"Today or tomorrow we will go to this or that city, spend a year there, carry on business and make money." Why, you do not even know what will happen tomorrow. What is your life? You are **a mist** that appears for a little while and then vanishes. Instead, you ought to say, "**If it is the Lord's will**, we will live and do this or that"* (James 4:13-15 NIV).

Most girls do not want to hear, *"If it is the Lord's will."* I am not advocating that you play "Deputy Downer" in your daughter's life after every date. But I *am* suggesting that you consider this special role of a loving spiritual monitor who is looking for the right time to mention this key: that only Papa God knows whether this is a lifelong love or a friendship "tutorial" in your daughter's understanding the difference between a Boaz and a Bozo, between Mr. Right and Mr. Wrong.

Although a present crush or dating relationship can evaporate like a mist just as quickly as it arrived, nothing is wasted in the emotional tutorial of a girl's heart.

Helping to Emotionally Constrain a Girl's Crushes

Moms need to carefully monitor their own careless comments about their daughter's boyfriends when they are tweens and teens. We need to teach our daughters the appropriate description of a boy they might know and enjoy being around. He is not a "boyfriend" but he is a friend who is a "boy." That simple distinction puts a boundary around the craziness that our society advocates through the media, 24/7.

We used this explanation so often around our house that I would often hear our daughter's friends say, "He is not a boyfriend, he is a boy who is a friend." Helping to emotionally constrain our daughters while they grow in patience is an emotional harness that will protect them immeasurably throughout high school and college and thereafter!

Moms also need to be more aware of the amount of time their daughters spend texting, e-mailing, or talking on the phone with particular guys! Bursting hormones without parallel maturity does not produce healthy boy-girl relating. That is why parents must cease and desist in making "foolish comments" about a certain guy being a future husband for their girl.

This all seems so innocent, and parents just having fun, but the by-product is not at all funny. I have seen captions under pictures on Facebook in which two five-year-olds (boy and girl) are hugging, and the parent writes: "My future daughter-in-law!"

To raise a Lady in Waiting, one must be a Mother in Waiting. The atmosphere created around girl-boy relationships should be as carefully cultivated in a girl's young life as it is when she hits puberty. And *that* is the parents' responsibility alone.

I know parents think such captions are just "cute," but the attitude is a reflection of a careless free-for-all that I constantly encounter in younger girls' lives. All the while I wonder, "Where is this child's parent?"

A parent of a sixth-grader read me a letter that her daughter wrote after being devastated by her "breakup" with a boy whom she had been "in love with" since fourth grade. The descriptives used in the letter were so deeply disturbing to me *because the emotions were so disproportionate to the reality of the relationship.* This precious young girl had lacked a spiritual monitor who could have characterized the reality of the friendship.

The emotional communication in the letter read like a woman who had been married for years and then betrayed by her beloved. I know that girls crushing on boys is normal, but this passionate heartbreak letter by a sixth-grader only fueled my heart's fire to warn moms against fanning the flames of "premature passion" in their daughters—literally passion that comes *before* maturity!

> TO RAISE A LADY IN WAITING, ONE MUST BE A MOTHER IN WAITING. THE ATMOSPHERE CREATED AROUND GIRL-BOY RELATIONSHIPS SHOULD BE AS CAREFULLY CULTIVATED IN A GIRL'S YOUNG LIFE AS IT IS WHEN SHE HITS PUBERTY.

Spiritual monitors are not just for young daughters; they are just as necessary for older single women. And listen, I confess that I too have been guilty about cheering too loud when one of my single friends had a date with a godly man!

I cheered too loud and too prematurely with one of my dearest single friends. When the glorious relationship burst into flames, the smoke choked not only the wonderful single gal but all those cheering on the sidelines. I asked this friend to forgive me and I still grieve today for allowing myself to be swept up in her enthusiasm. The crushing blow afterwards was almost a mortal wound emotionally. What is even sadder to me is that this particular single woman has taught the principle of the spiritual monitor as much as I have—but we both disregarded the principle amidst a flood of hope and passion.

> It is a mistaken idea—often shared by girls of all ages—that a wedding ring is a sort of magic token, a key that will unlock the door of happiness and at the same time end their problems. This can be true. But untold numbers of wives have found that a marriage not made in heaven can be next door to hell.[3]

Parents are often very invested in the development of certain skills in the lives of their children—academics, sports, music, dance—and dreaming of their kids' success. For a female, developing the skill of patience is as critical as mastering any skill. As I have said a thousand times, I have met too many girls who have mastered academics and the arts but have totally flunked in life! I know too many gifted girls who date Bozo guys and settle for so much less than God's best. We spend more time trying to pick out the right pair of jeans or the right prom dress for our daughters than we do tutoring the development of a patient Lady in Waiting who would attract a prince of a guy.

Dateless Friday nights are perfect times to encourage the development of patience. As dreadful as a "no plans with friends weekend" might seem, it is a great context for allowing God to develop your daughter's capacity to wait. My impulse as a mom was to try and rescue my daughter from a lonely weekend. Yet deep in my heart I knew that the vacuum in her heart needed God's touch and *not* Mama's trip-to-the-mall remedy.

Letter From Annie

This precious teen has had the most difficult year. Her family went through destructive flash floods and then a tornado several months later. I had sent her a copy of *Lady in Waiting* when she was fourteen. Recently I received a letter that revealed her as a teen learning about the word *wait*. Here is an excerpt from her sweet letter:

> ...I am learning how to be a living sacrifice. If only my friends knew how to WAIT on the Lord, they could be life-changers. My word to live by last year was HOPE, this year it is WAIT. I'm going to continue to WAIT on Him in my life so that I will renew my strength. As I WAIT for my Sweet Sixteenth birthday to come around, I am going to recklessly abandon myself to Him and wait on the one and only man He sends to me...Annie

Missed Out—While Waiting

My best friend was single until she was forty (yes!—a forty-year-old virgin). I have written about her in Chapter 3 of *Lady in Waiting*. During her prolonged, God-scripted singleness when she recounted to me about some

Bozo guy who hurt someone she knew, I would always respond, "Consider all the Bozo guys you have been *spared!*"

During her singleness, she witnessed so many tragic choices single women made, that her patience was actually strengthened by seeing so many "good" bad examples of what to avoid!

Recently another single friend, who is having a somewhat prolonged single journey, wrote about what she has *missed* while waiting for God's best and staying a virgin as she waits:

> [People] deeply underestimate the power of sex. It was not designed by God as a casual act to be shared indiscriminately with anyone and everyone. It was devised by our creator as the healthy byproduct of a healthy marriage, not the objective of a relationship. It was for this reason I made a commitment as a preteen to honor my future husband all the days of my life. I am still waiting, and when people suggest I have "missed out," I can agree:
>
> *I have missed out on heartbreak, insecurities relating to my body, sharing the most precious part of my heart with someone other than my husband, STDs, unplanned pregnancy, etc.* (emphasis added).[4]

Protected, Not Rejected

A recent post on Beth Moore's LPM blog by her Media Assistant, Lindsee Eddy, highlighted an incredibly important principle for any Young Lady in Waiting to fully grasp:

> What I do want you to know is that those boys not pursuing me is not a reflection of me whatsoever. It's not because I'm fat, or ugly, or don't dress cute enough, or am not outgoing enough, or am not godly enough, or whatever reason we girls can come up with. I truly believe it is the Lord protecting my heart.
>
> Although it could be easily labeled as rejection, it's simply the Lord's protection. At least that's how I've seen it.
>
> I don't know why He's chosen to protect my heart for so long. I do know that it's His grace in my life. I do know He alone has spared me from many broken hearts. I do know that He is building in me

something beautiful. I do know that He is sanctifying me through and through and molding me into the woman I am to be one day to my future husband. However future that may be. I do know that marriage is a legitimate desire of my heart that I believe He's placed there and that He will be faithful.

I might not be able to testify to the girls about the amazing man the Lord had blessed me with, but I am able to testify about His faithfulness despite my circumstances. He is good.

I know that I have rejected not one date, nor has the Lord ever rejected my heart, my desires, or me. And He won't reject yours, either.[5]

May God allow you to clearly see that you are a cheerleader for your daughter. One of your common cheers needs to be: "Sweetie, you are being protected not rejected!" Of course the primary cheer that all moms need to speak in prayer and throughout their encounters with their daughters and their friends is: "No Bozos! Only a Boaz!"

> MAY GOD ALLOW YOU TO CLEARLY SEE THAT YOU ARE A CHEERLEADER FOR YOUR DAUGHTER. ONE OF YOUR COMMON CHEERS NEEDS TO BE: "SWEETIE, YOU ARE BEING PROTECTED NOT REJECTED!"

Impatience and Aggressive Girls

The flip side to the issue of our girls being pursued by Bozos is the phenomenon of their pursuit of the guys! Whenever I teach on "Avoiding a Bozo," I am approached by mothers concerned about the "aggressive girls" who are pursuing their sons 24/7. Aggressive girls have always existed, but in case you are not aware of this, their tribe is increasing *at exponential rates*. We need to be aware of what is feeding the growth of this tribe!

Do you know when this phenomenon of aggressive girls began? Well, let's look right back to the Garden of Eden. When you consider what Eve did in The Garden and the far-reaching consequences of her aggressive choice, you can see that aggressive girls are just mini-Eves—I call them "Evettes."

I don't mean to simplify this reality, but the fuel behind a girl going after what her eyes desire is foundational to the existence of fallen humankind. To see something and then devise how to get it is utterly common behavior for the human heart.

> *Do not love the world or the things in the world....For all that is in the world—the desires of the flesh and the desires of the eyes and pride in possessions—is not from the Father but is from the world* (1 John 2:15-16 ESV).

Postponing one's desire or prayerfully submitting one's desire to God would sound ludicrous to a truly aggressive girl. Asking her to "wait" would be tortuous to her internal, demanding spirit. The sad reality of this aggressive lifestyle is the exhaustion that is its byproduct. As I have been saying to young women for thirty years: If you have to maneuver to get him, you'll have to maneuver to keep him—and that's exhausting.

Another motivation that drives aggressive girls is the pulsating love hunger in their hearts. We have addressed this love hunger in Chapter 7; you might remember the phrase "a compulsion for completion." This is a particular manifestation of that. Whenever I meet a girl who is in hot pursuit of a particular guy at her school, my heart grieves, because she has an insatiable appetite. This hunger drives little Evette to reach out and touch the forbidden fruit (in her case, most likely a Bozo guy).

This precious girl is unaware of her own hunger, and the corresponding hunger in Bozo guys for attention. Even if their compulsions arise from some legitimate need, by this point in their lives, those needs have become distorted.

During her hot pursuit of a guy she is majorly crushing on, the aggressive girl is living out the following quote by Dr. Leslie Parrott:

> If you try to build intimacy with another person before you have done the hard work of becoming whole on your own in Jesus, then all your relationships become an attempt to complete yourself, and it sets you up for failure.[6]

Another painful aspect behind the motive of an aggressive girl is the high probability of her being sexualized, or sexually stirred up. This has already been noted but can't be emphasized enough: Our society is sexualizing our children at an epidemic rate. Unfortunately, most of our children are not immunized against sexualized views of relationships. This subtle and not so subtle sexualization of our girls just feeds the idea of being aggressive. Add to the mix teen girlfriends who have also been sexualized; these girls cheer each other on in their aggressive daydreams!

Have you noticed in the 21st century that many popular TV shows have aggressive female leads accented with passive males? These role models can't help but encourage Evettes to go after their dreams—including Mr. Wonderful!

Being an Evette is ultimately the condition of all girls. Yet when this state develops into actual aggression, the aggressive girl's ability to operate freely is of the result of not having a spiritual monitor. When a girl has a spiritual monitor in her life, the monitor can shout when she reaches her hand toward the forbidden fruit!

I have spent decades shouting "Don't touch that tree!" to thousands of single girls. Without a spiritual monitor in the life of any single girl, teen or not, the aggressive tendency toward maneuvering and manipulating can guarantee her a Bozo match.

One other condition that often leads to aggressive behavior in girls is a home without a father. When the mother is the leader of a home, an aggressive female may be the role model a daughter sees every day.

Please understand, I have enormous respect for single moms and I *know* that it is a challenging job. A competent mother is such a blessing; but a controlling mother and/or a mother who is driven by her own hostility or fear can fuel aggression in her daughter. Moreover, a daughter who may be starved for male affirmation and attention is more likely to go looking for it in the form of unhealthy boys. These conditions will hasten her pilgrimage toward the Bozo tribe!

Besides "Sixteen," What Other Dating Prep Is Needed?

By the time you have read as far as this chapter, you know that this book is about preparing your daughter for the challenges of dating and finding her Boaz. Understanding the law of diminishing returns (see

Chapter 6) is the first requirement for a teen being prepared to date responsibly. Once your daughter understands this law, there are a few more guidelines for setting the parameters on when she is ready to date. Let's take a look.

Who Owns Your Body? (First Corinthians 6:19-20)

For any girl, young or not-so-young, the waiting period does not have to be wasted. The waiting for one's first date or one's first love is a time to evaluate your own personal strategy for moral purity. It is a time to really establish limits that allow you to be sexual, but holy. So, another critical prep for dating is for your daughter to set limits ahead of time—before she is tempted.

Below is a list to consider so that such limits can be clearly established *before* the temptation arrives.

> ANOTHER CRITICAL PREP FOR DATING IS FOR YOUR DAUGHTER TO SET LIMITS AHEAD OF TIME—BEFORE SHE IS TEMPTED.

Prior to her first date, any young woman should know this list as well as she knows her home address. These points are like the markings on her moral compass. Before she goes out the door of your home with a young man, she should have these in her heart as pre-temptation preparation:

1. How far would I go if Jesus were sitting next to me? (See Hebrews 4:13.)

2. What would a person I respect think of me? (See First Timothy 4:12.)

3. If we break up, can I look the other person in the eye? (See Acts 24:16.)

4. Do I feel guilty? (See Psalms 38:4.)

5. Does it turn me on sexually? (See First Peter 2:11.)

6. Would I want my parents to see what I am doing? (See Colossians 3:20.)

7. Would I want my future mate doing this right now? (See Hebrews 13:4.)

Another pre-temptation preparation is to realize when your girl may be most vulnerable sexually. Strengthening her moral compass as she daily faces our overly sexualized society is a gift better than tuition for college. So, as your girl's mother/mentor, this next little list (as well as the list above) is one to ponder—and to pray for the chance to share.

Vulnerable Situations, Sexually

1. Time: More time together, especially after 11 P.M.

2. Places: Too much time alone in a car (a hotel on wheels) or at home without parents

3. Positions: Lying together watching videos (stay upright)

4. Emotional events: Special occasions (prom), after a fight with parents, or following a great win or loss (with a sports team, for example)

Just being aware of these areas of vulnerability will keep you informed as a parent/mentor and prayerfully discerning on behalf of your girl. I often prayed about situations in which others laughed at my concerns.

Being a clueless parent can lead to disastrous things. Consider the cluelessness of King David in Second Samuel 13, in relation to the request of his firstborn son. King David was a clueless parent and the consequences were horrible.

I counseled a young woman who was molested at her neighbor's house after school, and asked her where her mom was at the time. Why would a mom allow a junior high girl to be in a house with older boys and no parental supervision?

This young woman said, "My mom was at work and it was after school." How ironic that parents are constantly scrambling for "child care" for their little ones after school, but totally miss the vulnerability of their hormonal tweens and teens after school!

Too many working moms are clueless about where their children actually are while they are at work. I wonder how many moms know that their young girls are playing next door where older boys are sometimes using their daughters like toys? I have counseled too many girls who were molested after school while hanging at friends' houses where older boys were also hanging out!

Impatience: The Pen Writing Post-Dated Checks for Marital Unfaithfulness

I met once with a single girl at Starbucks to discuss a few of her heart's questions. As I listened to her Mr. Bozo story, something she said sent me scrambling for a piece of paper to record it. This beautiful young woman explained, "I grew up being the good girl. I was a good girl in high school and a good girl in college. But after I graduated, *I violated my own values.*"

I asked her if she understood why she violated the values she had so strongly clung to all the way through school. Her immediate reply was, "Jackie, because of impatience with God, I felt that God had not delivered my Mr. Right...so I wasn't waiting any longer."

She described a relationship with a typical Bozo whom she knew deep in her heart was not God's best. She went on to elaborate on her rationalizing that other young people were living together. She thought, "So what is the big deal?"

Impatience propelled this young woman into the arms of a Bozo.

> THIS BEAUTIFUL YOUNG WOMAN EXPLAINED, "I GREW UP BEING THE GOOD GIRL. I WAS A GOOD GIRL IN HIGH SCHOOL AND A GOOD GIRL IN COLLEGE. BUT AFTER I GRADUATED, *I VIOLATED MY OWN VALUES.*"

Shortly after meeting with this young woman, I had lunch with another one who is gifted and bright and beautiful. She shared how frustrated she was that she didn't have her MRS. Degree yet! I warned her that her impatience would certify her vulnerability to become Bozo bait!

Here is a principle that so many young people want to remain oblivious to: the worst thing about having sex or fooling around physically before marriage is the vulnerability it leads to after marriage. When you fool around after marriage, it's even more costly. It's called adultery, and it wreaks havoc on marriages and families and even whole communities!

To remain pure prior to marriage is unquestionably a struggle, but young people think the struggle is because they're not married. What is so critical for our girls to understand is this: If you cannot control yourself sexually before marriage, you will likely not do so after marriage. I have never interviewed one person whose husband has been unfaithful who did not struggle and fool around with him before marriage. Sexual self-control is developed *this* side of marriage.

This is not to say that God cannot redeem sexual appropriateness within marriage for people who have been sexually active prior to matrimony. His grace enables us to grow in holiness at any stage of our spiritual development. But this takes intentional commitment and an understanding of how premarital sex affects the marriage relationship.

Without that conviction, however, sexual impurity before marriage is likely to be a post-dated check for immorality within marriage. That is called *adultery*. The gold ring on the left hand does not instantly transform us; we bring into marriage what we practiced before marriage.

Lest you're tempted to disregard the previous section as not being relevant to your daughter at her age, let me *shout this* to you from the page! The significance is just as relevant to your ten-year-old as it is to a single thirty-year-old, because the capacity to exhibit self-control is trained into your Young Lady of Patience from her earliest years.

By reading this book you are *way* ahead of the game in understanding this, I know, but I wouldn't have you deceived in any way about the impact of this principle.

Difference Between Lust and Love

As you work with your daughter to help teach her the many principles and practices of waiting, there is a critical distinction that she needs to understand about her potential for very strong feelings. In regards to her romantic attractions, she must comprehend the difference between lust and love.

This is a very confused topic in our culture. One of the most frustrating things about Hollywood is the portrayal of lust *as* love. These two words are not the same, yet they are often used as though they were synonyms. Lust is here today and gone tomorrow as the Bozo guy moves on to a new conquest. Lust is seeing something and setting one's heart upon it in pursuit. Lust can't wait to get, whereas love can wait to give. For lust, virtue and purity are very aggravating and exasperating, whereas for love, purity is captivating and inspiring. Lust is emotionally crippled by the limitations of passion. Couples who marry in passion alone may find that, when the passion subsides, their marriages end as quickly as their passion was sparked.

Teens who call sexual chemistry *love* rather than good ole lust are those who are rushing into either moving out of their homes to live with their boyfriends or fooling around in the backs of their cars. Like I wrote earlier, a car is just a hotel on wheels. These couples are having babies way before they have the maturity for the price-tag of parenting.

The patience that you encourage in your girl's heart will allow her to wait for "true love." True love requires a maturity and commitment that impatience has no tolerance for. Consider that the opening descriptive for *true love*— divinely inspired *agape*—is patience.

> *Love is patient and kind; love does not envy or boast; it is not arrogant or rude. It does not insist on its own way; it is not irritable or resentful... (1 Corinthians 13:4-5 ESV).*

Yes, in God's superlative definition for love, the first adjective given is *patient*. Lust cannot be patient, but is insistent on its own way. Lust fuels a war inside that harms, not only the heart of the one who lusts, but also the object of that lust.

Patiently Waiting: How Will I Know It is Him?

One day our daughter was wondering out loud "how she would know which guy was the best for her." I spontaneously shared the following and it has been shared with many others since. I told her that God's best for her would always complement the direction God wanted her to go. It is like a big running track with all these freshly painted lanes. As she takes off running in her lane, relentlessly in pursuit of Jesus, the guy who will complement her journey will arrive someday in this manner: She will be just running in her lane, looking ahead when all of a sudden she will hear this deep panting, and suddenly alongside her in the next lane she will hear someone approaching. She will not have to stop running, she will not have to change her pace, and she won't have to look behind her, because before she knows it, he will be running alongside her. He will keep up with her, and they will continue the race at a complementary pace. This will be her running partner for the journey ahead. They will encourage each other and not trip each other. I have met too many women who are running a fabulous race when suddenly they are tripped up by some Bozo guy shouting for her to slow down, take a break on the benches with him, and she is sidetracked for years by him.

Remember to be patient in anticipation of one coming up alongside you, who will also be panting in relentless pursuit of Jesus."[7]

Chapter 10—Questions for Discussion

1. Do you think your daughter is vulnerable to missionary dating? (See Second Corinthians 6:14.)

2. Are you a spiritual monitor for your daughter's crushes? (See Proverbs 13:20.)

3. How patient is your teen? Is *wait* a cuss word to her? (See Isaiah 64:4.)

4. Discuss the blog, "I've Rejected Not One," and the idea that our daughters' datelessness is protection from many Bozo wounds. (See Ruth 2:8-9.)

5. Discuss "aggressive girls" and some of the *whys* behind their behavior, including maneuvering to get and maneuvering to keep.

6. Discuss the dating rules for your family.

7. Discuss the lists about the readiness of teens to date.

8. Discuss the idea that impatience is the pen that writes post-dated checks for marital unfaithfulness.

9. Do you and your daughter know the difference between *lust* and *love?* Discuss and consider the *true love* list below, after reading First Corinthians 13:4-8:

   - True love distinguishes between a person and a body.

   - True love always generates respect.

   - True love is self-giving.

   - True love can thrive without physical expression.

   - True love seeks to build relationship.

   - True love embraces responsibility.

   - True love can postpone gratification.

   - True love is a commitment.

CHAPTER 11

P. S.:
Final Words for Mom

As I thought about the things I wanted to cover in this final chapter, I had to laugh, because the image that came to mind was a bunch of Tupperware containers filled with "leftovers" after a holiday. The leftovers from this feast are in print, but the "containers" hold specific foods for specific situations that moms may face on their journey. You might not need the information right at this moment, but you will need it eventually.

You can read this whole chapter or skim for a Tupperware container with exactly what your soul has been hungry for. Each container will be labeled with a question. Pick what you need and leave the other containers for future reference!

Mom, Do You Feel Like a Failure Today?

If you have finished this book and are now struggling with doubts or feelings of inadequacy as a mom, *please* go back and reread the disclaimer at the end of the Introduction!

We are all pilgrims on this journey and it is *only* in clinging to Jesus that we can parent our girls. Did you know that there are more verses in the Bible on treating skin disease than on raising children? A great book to encourage you when you are tempted to seek formulaic answers to your parenting struggle is by Leslie Leyland Fields. It is entitled *Parenting Is Your Highest Calling and 8 Other Myths That Trap Us in Worry and Guilt*. When I finished reading this book, I was as giddy as a little girl on Christmas morning.

Would You Like to Lead a *Lady in Waiting* Group?

You can lead a group for your daughter and her friends in your home! For twenty-two years, precious women have taken others through *Lady in Waiting*. Here are some simple steps to follow as the leader:

1. Read *Lady in Waiting* and answer the questions at the end of each chapter.

2. The new edition of *Lady in Waiting* includes a very detailed workbook. Honestly, though, many people find that reading the book and answering the chapter questions is sufficient.

3. If after reading each chapter and answering the questions you want more information, you can work through the workbook at the back of the book.

4. Many young women and moms have held summer Bible studies for teens, and taken them through the book. Each participant buys a copy of *Lady in Waiting*; the chapters are short, so the book can be covered in ten weeks, or doubled up in five weeks. When the book study takes place during the school year, the pace can match that of the girls' calendar.

5. A girl can participate even if she hasn't read the chapter; she can certainly find the discussion of the material helpful. Many times this is used in Sunday school; visitors can always comprehend the principles because they are based so deeply on the Book of Ruth. In *Lady in Waiting* each chapter stands on its own; a girl can miss a week and still understand the discussion when she returns.

6. On my web site is a DVD in the Products section titled *No Bozo*. It is often shown at the end of the Bible study series or

even at the beginning to expose the need for studying *Lady in Waiting*. On the DVD are two messages: one from 1994 and one from 2004. The one from 2004 is excellent for every age, especially teens; the 1994 message was filmed in front of older singles and is a great refresher of the book *Lady in Waiting* for the teacher.

7. Remember, the best teacher is the one who processes the material first and then takes others through it.

A half million single women of all ages have studied *Lady in Waiting* in Bible study groups. If you plan to do this, you are continuing a nation-wide—even international—tradition. It's like a rite of passage for single women who wish to challenge themselves and others not to settle, but to wait for God's best—and *avoid Bozos!*

Have You Minimized Your Daughter's Pain?

Don't minimize a teen's pain/discontentment/abandonment since time doesn't heal all wounds.

People may say that time heals all wounds, but if someone has not done the hard work of forgiveness, time only moves the pain below the surface. So often a person will say, "It hurts too much to feel the pain again."

My reply is "It hurts more *not* to feel it." The insidious crime of rape is not what ultimately kills the soul; it is the shaming silence a woman lives with, often for *years*, that holds her hostage to the deep offense. Sexual abuse is a soul-deadening crime not only because of the violent, dishonoring physical treatment, but also because of the shame that keeps the victim silent.

A dear friend from college sent me some of her counseling notes years ago:

Deal with incest, abuse, etc., in therapy by:

- Allowing the victims to tell their stories.
- Allowing the victims to grieve.
- Helping victims make new decisions—who they are now, etc.
- Helping them to have new experiences.

These notes are so simple and yet so profound. If God's children would just learn to allow the offended to tell their stories and *grieve* the offenses, there would be far less spiritual illness in the Body of Christ.

When pain is buried, it is buried only for a time. When it comes to the surface of one's life—and it *will* come to the surface—it often erupts in destructive behaviors that could have been prevented had the person been able to sufficiently grieve the offense, loss, or devastation.

In his tragedy, *Macbeth,* Shakespeare wisely recommended, "Give sorrow words. The grief that does not speak whispers the o're-fraught heart and bids it break."

Time does heal, but time heals only the wounds we allow the light of God to shine on and expose. Time ferments and intensifies wounds that are hidden; but God wants us to come to Him with all this pain. Too often we don't face our pain because we are too scared. Sometimes we don't think God will be able to comfort us adequately, but we need to give Him a chance. In truth, He is more than able!

Blessed be the God and Father of our Lord Jesus Christ, the Father of mercies and God of all comfort, who comforts us in all our affliction, so that we may be able to comfort those who are in any affliction, with the comfort with which we ourselves are comforted by God (2 Corinthians 1:3-4 ESV).

Can You Help Me?
A Girl Has Been Sexually Abused!

Each of my children had friends who had experienced the soul-deadening crime of sexual abuse. God used our family through prayer and guiding them toward professional counseling.

Here are some steps you can take and a resource that you and the victim can access for free right now:

1. Go to www.jackiekendall.com.

2. Click on the FAQs tab on the menu bar of the home page.

3. Click on the first line: "How does one recover from Sexual Abuse?"

4. Click on the box that reads "Recovery from Sexual Abuse," and the radio interview will begin.

5. Here, you can listen to a short but powerful message of *hope:* Out of something painful, something beautiful can grow! This message is an interview in which I share how I have gone from victim to victory!

Prior to speaking at a large mother-daughter conference, I was told that several of the young girls who would be attending had been molested by a staff member. The staff member would be going to trial in the next two weeks, so the past wounds were being freshly confronted.

The morning of the event, I came across the story of Jarius' daughter, whom Jesus called back to life after she died: *"Talitha koum!"* (Mark 5:41 NIV).

Immediately the Lord spoke to my heart and said, *"Today, Jackie, you are going to call some young girls back from the dead."*

At the conference, as each mother brought her daughter up to me, I prayed over each girl that Jesus would heal her heart wound, and call her back from the emotionally deadening experience of abuse. Jarius' daughter was twelve years old when she was raised from the dead, and most of the little girls I prayed with were seventh-graders, twelve and thirteen years old.

In the first Scripture passage that Jesus read publicly, He said He came to *"heal the brokenhearted"* (Luke 4:18 NKJV). Isaiah also referred to Jesus as being *"familiar with suffering"* (Isa. 53:3 NIV). Jesus' familiarity with suffering allows Him to heal the brokenhearted; my familiarity with suffering allows me to be a wounded healer, and a healed forgiver, in His name.

JESUS' FAMILIARITY WITH SUFFERING ALLOWS HIM TO HEAL THE BROKENHEARTED; MY FAMILIARITY WITH SUFFERING ALLOWS ME TO BE A WOUNDED HEALER, AND A HEALED FORGIVER, IN HIS NAME.

Then the Lord reminded me of a term I found while researching the name *Yeshua*—friend of the brokenhearted (see Ps. 34:18). In Acts 1:24, the Greek term is *kardiognostes*, meaning "a heart-knower."[1] The minute I remembered this term, I saw my hand over my heart in a pledge, which would be a daily whispered prayer: "*Kardiognostes*, heal my heart wounds."

I told each girl to place her hand over her heart and continually whisper this prayer to Jesus: "Heal my heart wound, Lord." The healing of such a wound takes time; I know this all too well.

At the end of the conference, as I was sitting alone at the airport, I placed my hand over my heart and pledged a new allegiance to the One who is the ultimate Healer of heart wounds. While my hand was over my heart, I thanked God for the abuse that I had lived through as a child, because the suffering I had experienced became the very platform of hope that Jesus can use to call a person back from "the soul-deadening experience of sexual abuse." Before you go to sleep tonight, place your hand over your heart and ask Jesus to heal any fresh or old heart wound.

*If we are distressed, it is **for your comfort and salvation*** (2 Corinthians 1:6).

Those Struggling to Listen to Papa

Remember the story in Chapter 1 about the Jewish girl listening to her Papa? I have found a particular group of women and girls who have the most difficult time listening to Papa. The difficulty is not because they are being particularly stubborn. It is because they find it hard to listen to their heavenly Papa after being so deeply wounded by their earthly papas.

Recently, Ken was on the phone talking with a woman who needed guidance for her niece who had just been molested. At the same moment, I was e-mailing an abuse victim whom I directed to go to my web site and listen to "Recovery from Sexual Abuse" online. If you know someone who isn't able to listen to Papa at this time because of her "papa wound," encourage her to do the following:

1. Go to www.jackiekendall.com.

2. Click on the FAQs tab on the menu bar of the home page.

3. Click on the first line: "How does one recover from Sexual Abuse?"

4. Click on the box that reads "Recovery from Sexual Abuse," and the radio interview will begin.

Help! I Found Porn on My Child's Computer!

The following suggestions are from Vicki Courtney, who is the go-to expert on so many topics. When I read this blog post, I knew it needed to be included in this section on porn. I used to think of porn as being isolated to boys only; I am daily surprised by the increase of girls visiting such sites. God have mercy on our children!

Vicki's suggestions are fabulous:

Put safety filters on your home computers and deactivate the web browser on your children's handheld devices. If you feel your child is old enough to access the web on the home computer, add monitoring software to spot-check their web activity. If they are accessing the web on handheld devices, make it a practice to spot-check their devices from time to time. The rule of thumb in our home was: If I don't have the time to monitor the device, it's not a good time for my child to have it. It's important that we let your children know that our ultimate goal is to protect them from 1) outside influences that can have long-term results and 2) themselves. We all make mistakes and our children are no different.

Help your children come up with an escape plan. It's not a matter of "if," but "when" your children will be exposed to pornography, whether they stumble upon it with an accidental click, seek it out on their own, or are introduced to it by someone they know. Help them come up with what they might say if they are at a friend's house or in a situation where they unexpectedly find themselves on the receiving end of peer pressure. Encourage them to let you know when this happens and assure them that this is a welcome topic in your home.

Educate your children about the long-term effects of viewing pornography. I give an overview of the damaging effects in 5 Conversations

You Must Have With Your Son as well as introduce a helpful tool to encourage self control: STP (Stop, Think, Pray). If your son is ten or older, it's time to brush up on Conversation #2 and present the truths in a way that will respect his age and level of understanding. If your son is under 10 but has been exposed to a more worldly environment (younger child in family, attends public school, plays on rec/sports teams with older boys, etc.), you may need to begin this conversation sooner.

Put it on your calendar to talk about this topic at least once every two months. The information presented is more likely to be absorbed by your child with repetition. You can assign this task to one parent or share in the responsibility. In my home, I had the majority of the conversations related to this topic, since I spent more time with the children during the day. However, my husband was also vigilant in taking our sons through the book, "Preparing Your Son for Every Man's Battle" and encouraging them to meet with an accountability partner (which both my sons do), who will ask them some tough questions (and vice versa).[2]

Additional resources:

1. *Wired for Intimacy: How Pornography Hijacks the Male Brain* by William Struthers.

2. http://www.pornharms.com/

How Should I Handle Same-Sex Experimentation?

I have lived on this earth long enough to be able to agree wholeheartedly with Solomon when he penned the words under the inspiration of God's Spirit, "there is nothing new under the sun." Yet, even knowing this, there may be things in each generation that seem new. What I want to write about here is unquestionably in that category.

In a book encouraging you to raise daughters who are equipped in the Lord to walk in purity of mind and body and to wait on His best for their lives, I would be selling you short by not bringing some attention to a category of sexual saturation and temptation in our culture that has exploded in the past decade or so: same-sex attraction.

Just like the moms of the 1950s who may have wanted to imagine that there was no premarital sex happening on their watch, we would be in complete denial if we didn't realize that there is actual pressure in the culture for young people to "experiment" with same-gender sexuality.

That pressure comes from our entertainment media and it comes from their peers in school—including Christian schools! There is not only acceptance of same-sex activity; there is also accessibility in the form of young people who have been convinced that this is just another choice in the cafeteria of romance.

So moms, *please stay awake!* If you don't understand that your daughter or her friends can be as vulnerable in this area as they are in any area of disordered affections, you are kidding yourself. Emotionally- and physically-developing young people can be very susceptible to pressure; they can also be confused by mixing emotional desires with sexual ones.

We now see an entire generation of kids who have been taught, at least outside the home, that same-sex activity is normative. For young girls, this can be complicated by their *natural* affection and affinity for one another. They are given the message that such heart affection *must* be sexual or *could* be. Like the pressure from Bozo guys, heart-wounded girls can try to push their friends into the physical realm.

If you suspect your daughter is confused emotionally or even inclined physically toward another girl, of course the first thing you want to do is to pray and ask for wisdom! This is certainly an area where a parent is wise to seek godly, Christian counsel, because such confusion around emotional and sexual attraction can be complex. The kind of intervention would depend on how far along the continuum someone is—from a crush stage to finding out a daughter is actually involved with another girl. What a parent might do would then vary accordingly.

As with crushes and attraction to boys, one of the *most* important qualities parents can apply to navigating this territory of a girl's heart (after prayerfulness) is calm and loving attention. Your kitchen table or family room couch or the edge of her bed—wherever you have your most heartfelt talks—should be the safest place in her life.

Additional Resources:
Suggestions for Research and Counseling

1. http://exodusinternational.org/

2. http://samesexattraction.org/

3. *Setting Love in Order: Hope and Healing for the Homosexual* by Mario Bergner

Final Words

I am having separation anxiety as I finish this book. The anxiety flows from wanting to be sure that I have shared every aspect of my soul on this topic with you. I want to make sure I have given you thorough "Cliff's Notes" on each aspect of raising a Young Lady in Waiting. This morning the Lord reminded me that He has provided you and me with the ultimate instruction manual. Here is a reminder that God has given you and me all the "Cliff's Notes" we need:

> *For whatever was written in former days was written for our instruction, that through endurance and through the encouragement of the Scriptures we might have hope* (Romans 15:4 ESV).

A Peak at My Library and Quiet-Time Habits

We are the sum total of what we have read. Here are some suggestions for excellent reading and studying:

Bible Study Helps

- Best: *Hebrew Greek Key Word Study Bible* (NIV) (An expensive item, but a great investment)

- *The One Year Bible* (A format for consistency in daily reading)

- Different translations: *Phillips, Amplified, NIV, The Message,* and *New Living Translation*

- Also, *Strong's Exhaustive Concordance* (For looking up words in the original Hebrew or Greek)

- And, a personal journal to record the daily nuggets you receive (see Isa. 50:4)

Trust Building

Activity:

- Take a red pen, read through the Book of Psalms, and underline the word *trust* wherever it appears.

Read:

- *Trusting God* by Jerry Bridges
- *Disappointment With God* by Philip Yancey
- *In the Eye of the Storm* by Max Lucado
- *Finding God* by Dr. Larry Crabb
- *Through Gates of Splendor* by Elisabeth Elliot
- *Passion & Purity* by Elisabeth Elliot
- *Shattered Dreams* by Dr. Larry Crabb
- *The Legacy of Sovereign Joy* by John Piper
- *Crazy Love* by Francis Chan

Prayer

Activity:

- Make prayer lists on 3 x 5 cards and carry them in your purse for using whenever you have to wait somewhere.

Read:

- *What Happens When Women Pray* by Evelyn Christenson
- *Fresh Wind, Fresh Fire* by Jim Cymbala
- *Handle With Prayer* by Charles Stanley
- *A Hunger for God* by John Piper
- *Don't Waste Your Life* by John Piper

Devotion to God

Read:

- *A Chance to Die* by Elisabeth Elliot

- *My Utmost, for His Highest* by Oswald Chambers
- *The Christian's Secret of a Happy Life* by Hannah W. Smith; also Hannah's biography
- *Soul Care* by Peter Lord
- *Abba's Child* by Brennan Manning
- *The Furious Longing of God* by Brennan Manning
- *Celebration of Discipline* by Richard Foster
- *Pursuit of God* by A.W. Tozer
- *Knowing God* by J.I. Packer
- *31 Days of Praise* by Ruth Meyers
- *The Path of Loneliness and How to Overcome Loneliness* by Elisabeth Elliot
- *100 Christian Women Who Changed the 20th Century* by Helen Kooiman Hosier
- *Spiritual Classics* by Richard Foster & Emilie Griffin
- *Tale of Three Kings* by Gene Edwards
- *Waking the Dead* by John Eldredge
- *Renovation of the Heart* by Dallas Willard
- *The Dangerous Duty of Delight* by John Piper
- *A Hunger for God* by John Piper
- *Desiring God* by John Piper
- *A Resilient Life* by Gordon MacDonald
- *Counterfeit Gods* by Timothy Keller
- Any books by Beth Moore or Anne Graham Lotz

God's Will

Read:

- *Found: God's Will* by John MacArthur

- *The Normal Christian Life* by Watchman Nee
- *True Spirituality* by Francis Schaeffer
- *The Root of Righteousness* by A.W. Tozer
- *Exquisite Agony* by Gene Edwards
- *Tale of Three Kings* by Gene Edwards
- *A Man Worth Waiting For* by Jackie Kendall

Grace

Read:

- *What's So Amazing About Grace?* by Philip Yancey
- *Ragamuffin Gospel* by Brennan Manning
- *Freedom From the Performance Trap* by David Seamands
- *Redeeming Love* by Francine Rivers (fiction)
- *12 Steps for the Recovering Pharisee (like me)* by Jon Fischer
- *The Grace Awakening* by Chuck Swindoll

Self-Image & Emotional Soul Care

Read:

- *Free Yourself to Love: The Liberating Power of Forgiveness* by Jackie Kendall
- *The Search for Significance* by Robert McGee
- *Shame and Grace* by Lewis Smedes
- *Inside Out* by Dr. Larry Crabb
- *The Blessing* by Gary Smalley and John Trent
- *Boundaries* by Dr. Henry Cloud and Dr. John Townsend
- *A Way of Seeing* by Edith Schaeffer
- *L'Abri* by Edith Schaeffer
- *The World According to Me* by Sandra Wilson (control)

- *Calm My Anxious Heart* by Linda Dillow

Parenting

Read:

- *The Mentoring Mom* by Jackie Kendall
- *Lady in Waiting for Little Girls by Jackie Kendall* (a mother-daughter devotional activity book, ages 4-10)
- *The Key to Your Child's Heart* by Gary Smalley
- *Kids in Danger* by Dr. Ross Campbell (anger)
- *Parenting With Love & Logic* by Foster Cline and Jim Fay
- *When You Feel Like Screaming* by Pat Holt and Grace Ketterman
- *The Treasure Tree* by Gary Smalley and John Trent
- *Families Where Grace Is In Place* by Jeffrey VanVonderen
- *Parenting Isn't For Cowards* by James Dobson
- *The Strong-Willed Child* by James Dobson
- *Lady in Waiting* by Debby Jones and Jackie Kendall (parenting teen girls)
- *Parenting Is Your Highest Calling and 8 Other Myths That Trap Us in Worry and Guilt* by Leslie Fields

Marriage

Read:

- *Saving Your Marriage Before It Starts* by Drs. Les and Leslie Parrott
- *Love & Respect* by Dr. Emerson Eggerichs
- *The God Empowered Wife* by K.B. Haught
- *His Needs, Her Needs* by Dr. W. Harley
- *The 5 Love Languages* by Gary Chapman

- *Toward a Growing Marriage* by Gary Chapman
- *Intimate Issues* by Linda Dillow
- *Fool-Proofing Your Life* by Jan Silvious
- *Incompatibility: Still Grounds for a Great Marriage* by Chuck and Barb Snyder
- *Every Man's Battle* by Steve Arterburn
- *The Blessing* by Gary Smalley and John Trent
- *Shattered Dreams* by Dr. Larry Crabb
- *Rescue Your Love Life* by Dr. Henry Cloud and Dr. John Townsend
- *What Did You Expect?* by Paul Tripp
- *Not Just Friends* by Shirley P. Glass

Sexual Issues

Read:

- *Eros Defiled and Eros Redeemed* by John White
- *An Affair of the Mind* by Laurie Hall (addiction)
- *Every Man's Battle* by Steve Arterburn

Marital Affairs

Read:

- *Torn Asunder: Recovering From Extramarital Affairs* by Dave Carder
- *Love Must Be Tough* by James Dobson
- *Hope for the Separated* by Gary Chapman
- *An Affair of the Mind* by Laurie Hall

Sexual Abuse

Read:

- *Outgrowing the Pain* by Eliana Gil

- *The Wounded Heart* by Dan Allender
- *No Place to Cry* by Doris VanStone and Erwin Lutzer

Christian Fiction

Read:

- *Redeeming Love* by Francine Rivers (fiction)
- Any books by Bodie and Brock Thoene

Public Speaking Preparation

Read:

- *Teaching to Change Lives* by Dr. Howard Hendricks

Endnotes

Preface

1. "Henry Ward Beecher Quotes," ThinkExist.com, http:// thinkexist.com/quotation/the_mother-s_heart_is_the_ child s_schoolroom/153259.html (accessed September 24, 2012).

2. "George Herbert Palmer Quotes," goodreads.com, http://www. goodreads.com/quotes/192078-one-good-mother-is-worth-a-hundred-schoolmasters (accessed September 24, 2012).

3. Steve Wright with Chris Graves, *A Parent Privilege,* by (Wake Forest, NC: InQuest Publishing, 2008), 18.

Chapter 1: Raising a Young Lady of Reckless Abandon

1. C.S. Lewis, *Mere Christianity* (New York: HarperCollins, 2001), 198.

2. Ibid.

Chapter 2: Raising a Young Lady of Diligence

1. Katie Davis, *Kisses from Katie: A Story of Relentless Love and Redemption* (New York: Simon & Schuster, Inc, 2011), xi.

2. Rhonda Grant, Facebook post.

3. Larry Crabb, *Encouragement:The Key to Caring* (Grand Rapids: Zondervan Publishing House, 1984), 10.

4. Biblesoft's New Exhaustive Strong's Numbers and Concordance with Expanded Greek-Hebrew Dictionary, CD-ROM, Biblesoft, Inc. and International Bible Translators, Inc. (1994, 2003, 2006) s.v. "sumpatheo," (NT 4834).

5. Katie Davis, *Kisses from Katie,* xi.

Chapter 3: Raising a Young Lady of Faith

1. *Brown-Driver-Briggs Hebrew and English Lexicon, Unabridged,* Electronic Database, Biblesoft, Inc. (2002, 2003, 2006), s.v. "Boaz" (OT 1162).

2. Biblesoft's New Exhaustive Strong's Numbers and Concordance with Expanded Greek-Hebrew Dictionary, CD-ROM, Biblesoft, Inc. and International Bible Translators, Inc. (1994, 2003, 2006) s.v. "shanan," (OT 8150).

3. *Oxford Dictionaries,* April 2010, Oxford University Press, s.v. "inculcate," http://oxforddictionaries.com/definition/american_english/inculcate (accessed September 20, 2012).

4. Ibid.

5. One of my mentors, M.E. Cravens, a statement made in 1975. Also, see my book, *The Mentoring Mom* (Birmingham, AL: New Hope Publishers, 2006), 68.

6. Sally Lloyd-Jones, *The Jesus Storybook Bible* (Grand Rapids: Zondervan Publishers, 2007), 137.

7. Beth Moore, *So Long Insecurity: You've Been a Bad Friend to Us* (Carol Stream, IL: Tyndale House Publishers, 2010), 342.

8. Courtney Veseay, e-mail message to author.

Chapter 4: Raising a Young Lady of Virtue

1. Merriam-Webster Online, *Merriam-Webster Online Dictionary 2012,* s.v. "virtue," http://www.merriam-webster.com/dictionary/virtue (accessed September 27, 2012).

2. Kate Elizabeth Conner, "Ten Things I Want to Tell Teenage Girls" Lily Pads,/March 25, 2012 http://kateelizabethconner. com/?s=Ten+Things+I+Want+to+Tell+Teenage+Girls& Submit (accessed September 27, 2012). Kate is the mom of two toddlers.

3. Elizabeth Holmes, "For Prom, Schools Say 'No' to the Dress," Wall Street Journal, March 25, 2012, http://online.wsj.com/article/SB10001424052702303816504577309532960793266.html (accessed September 20, 2012).

4. "Dispatches/Quotables," *World Magazine*, February 25, 2012, 16.

5. Biblesoft's New Exhaustive Strong's Numbers and Concordance with Expanded Greek-Hebrew Dictionary, CD-ROM, Biblesoft, Inc. and International Bible Translators, Inc. (1994, 2003, 2006) s.v. "chamad," (OT 2530).

6. International Standard Bible Encyclopedaeia, *International Standard Bible Encyclopaedia*, Electronic Database, Biblesoft, Inc. (1995-1996, 2003), s.v. "Hananiah."

7. *Easton's Bible Dictionary*, PC Study Bible formatted electronic database, Biblesoft, Inc. (2003, 2006), s.v. "Mishael."

8. Ibid, s.v. "Azariah."

Chapter 5: Raising a Young Lady of Devotion

1. A.W. Tozer, *The Root of the Righteous* (Camp Hill, PA: Christian Publishing, Inc., 1985), 5.

2. Eric Metaxas, *Bonhoeffer: Pastor, Martyr, Prophet, Spy* (Nashville: Thomas Nelson 2010), 14.

3. Paul Tripp, *What Did You Expect?* (Wheaton, IL: Crossway, 2010), 22.

4. David Platt, *Radical: Taking Back Your Faith from the American Dream* (Colorado Springs: Multnomah Books, 2010), 7.

5. C.V., personal note to author, July 2010.

Chapter 7: Raising a Young Lady of Security

1. Christina Stolass, "A Radiant Reflection," MadHattin Mom, blog post April 20, 2012, http://madhattinmom.com/to-be-radiant/ (accessed September 21, 2012).

2. Dr. Susie Orbach, Activity Sheet 2.2 courtesy of the Dove Campaign for Real Beauty (accessed January 2007), as noted in: Shelly Ballestero, *Beauty by God* (Ventura, CA: Regal Books, 2009), 18.

3. Spiros Zodhiates, ThD, *Hebrew-Greek Key Study Bible* (Chattanooga: AMG Publishers, 1996), 1679).

4. Jerry Bridges, *Trusting God Even When Life Hurts* (Colorado Springs, CO: NavPress, 1988), 155.

5. Beth Moore, *So Long Insecurity: You've Been a Bad Friend to Us* (Carol Stream, IL: Tyndale House Publishers, 2010), xiii.

6. Donald Miller, *To Own a Dragon* (Colorado Springs, CO: NavPress, 2006), 139, 140.

7. Melissa Trevathan and Sissy Goff, *All You Need to Know About Raising Girls* (Grand Rapids: Zondervan, 2007), 69.

8. Kristi Nolan, e-mail to the author.

9. Melissa Trevathan and Sissy Goff, *All You Need to Know About Raising Girls*, 155.

Chapter 8: Raising a Young Lady of Contentment

1. John W. Gardner, Facebook post, July 22, 2012.

2. Horace Mann quoted in Richard A. Swenson, M.D., *A Minute of Margin*, (Colorado Springs: NavPress, 2003), front matter.

3. Lloyd Ogilvie, *The Bush Is Still Burning* (Waco, TX: Word Books, 1980), 159.

4. Ibid.

5. See Anne Lamott, *Blue Shoe* (New York: Riverhead Books, 2002), 136.

6. Adapted from Jackie Kendall, *Free Yourself to Love* (Nashville: FaithWords, 2008) 186,187.

7. Linda Dillow, *Calm My Anxious Heart* (Colorado Springs, CO: NavPress, 2007), 13.

8. Robert Lupton, "The Wrong and Right Ways to Help," *World Magazine*, July 14, 2012, 43.

9. John MacArthur, *The MacArthur Daily Bible*, (Nashville: Thomas Nelson, 2003), 418.

10. Linda Dillow, *Calm My Anxious Heart*, 13.

Chapter 9: Raising a Young Lady of Conviction

1. The Bozo/Boaz comparison is adapted from subtitles in Chapter 6 of my book, *A Man Worth Waiting For* (Nashville: FaithWords, 2008).

2. John Adams, as quoted in Jackie Kendall, *A Man Worth Waiting For* (Nashville: FaithWords, 2008), 191.

3. Donald Miller, *To Own a Dragon* (Colorado Springs, CO: NavPress, 2006), 139.

4. List adapted from: Jackie Kendall and Debby Jones, *Lady in Waiting: Becoming God's Best While Waiting for Mr. Right* (Shippensburg, PA: Destiny Image, 2005), 127-128.

5. Ibid., 129.

6. List adapted from: Jackie Kendall and Debby Jones, *Lady in Waiting*, 127-128.

Chapter 10: Raising a Young Lady of Patience

1. Pamela Druckerman, "Why French Parents Are Superior," *The Wall Street Journal*, wsj.com, February 4, 2012, http://online.wsj.com/article/SB10001424052970204740904577196931457473816.html (accessed September 21, 2012).

2. Ibid.

3. Dr. Clyde Narramore, *Dating* (Zondervan Publications, 1961), 17.

4. Esther Fleece, "The Temptation of Tim Tebow," *The Washington Post*, April 26, 2012. (Esther is Assistant to the President for Millennial Relations at Focus on the Family.)

5. Lindsee Eddy, "I've Rejected Not One," LPM blog (Living Proof Ministries) August 2, 2012, http://blog.lproof.org/2012/08/ive-rejected-not-one.html (accessed September 22, 2012).

6. Jackie Kendall, *A Man Worth Waiting For* (Nashville: FaithWords, 2008), 182.

7. Adapted from: Jackie Kendall, *A Man Worth Waiting For* (Nashville: FaithWords, 2008), 25-26.

Chapter 11: P.S.: Final Words for Mom

1. Biblesoft's New Exhaustive Strong's Numbers and Concordance with Expanded Greek-Hebrew Dictionary, CD-ROM, Biblesoft, Inc. and International Bible Translators, Inc. (1994, 2003, 2006) s.v. "kardiognostes," (NT 2589).

2. Blog excerpt: Vicki Courtney, "Some scary new porn statistics," May 1, 2012, Vicki Courtney, http://vickicourtney.com/?s=may+1%2C+2012 (accessed September 22, 2012).

About Jackie Kendall

Jackie Kendall has been a sought-after conference speaker for thirty-five years. As president of Power to Grow Ministries, Jackie speaks to people of all ages and stages of life (including, since 1992, professional baseball and football players). Jackie is the author of several books, and the co-author of the bestselling *Lady in Waiting*.

For speaking engagements
or to get more information, contact Jackie at:

POWER TO GROW MINISTRIES
www.jackiekendall.com

JOIN THE
MOVEMENT

WITH JACKIE KENDALL

Get the
Raising a Lady in Waiting Study Course
for your family, home-school group,
or church today!

www.RaisingaLadyinWaiting.com